restoring the color of roses

restoring the color of roses

barrie jean borich

Firebrand
Books
Ithaca, New York

Portions of this book appeared in *Hurricane Alice* and in *Wordsworth*, the literary supplement to the *Minnesota Daily*.

Book design by Betsy Bayley
Cover design by Lee Tackett
Cover floral image adapted from work by Christina Bates
Typesetting by Bets Ltd.

Printed in the United States on acid-free paper by McNaughton & Gunn

Author's Note:
Without imagination, memory has no substance. While the stories told here are autobiographical, some of the characters and events are composites. The writing of this book has been a collaboration of memory and imagination, in search of the emotional, if not always a literal, truth.

Library of Congress Cataloging-in-Publication Data

Borich, Barrie Jean, 1959–
    Restoring the color of roses / by Barrie Jean Borich.
      p.   cm.
    ISBN 1-56341-028-1 (hard : alk. paper). — ISBN 1-56341-027-3 (pbk. : alk. paper)
    1. Lesbians—Illinois—Chicago—Literary collections.   I. Title.
PS3552.07529R47   1993
813'.54—dc20   93-647
                                              CIP

acknowledgments

I'd like to thank all the people who helped me throughout the writing of this book. These people include: my handsome lover, Linnea Stenson, who has been a true partner; Judith Katz who was always there to tell me what was going to happen next in the publishing process; T.C. Largaespada who read the first draft and from that point on acted as if the book was already published; Chris Cinque who has always understood what I was trying to do; Peter Farstad who always laughed in the right places; Lisa Berg and Gretchen Legler who read early drafts and who, along with Jennifer Juárez Robles, helped me proof the galleys; Morgan Grayce Willow and Ellen Lansky who marked up the final draft; all the Berthas that I've worked with over time, especially the most recent gang which includes some of the women listed above as well as Lynette D'Amico, Susan Rothbaum, and Ann Rickertson; Patrick Scully for his Cabaret; and Alexs Pate who has thrown a number of opportunities my way and who is consistently willing to help build alliances between straight African-Americans and white Queers.

I also want to thank all the teachers, students, and coworkers in the Program in Creative and Professional Writing and other University of Minnesota hot spots who supported this project in its earlier forms: Terri Whitman, Mary Petrie, Solomon Deressa,

Patricia Hampl, Mimi Sprengnether, Cathy Coskran, Toni McNaron, Robin Brown, Paulette Bates Alden, Michael Dennis Browne, Charlie Sugnet, Chris Mack Gordon, and all the others I'm forgetting. And thanks to: all the teachers who influenced me including Gloria Anzaldúa, Olga Broumas, Carolyn Forché, and Jim Moore; all my students over the last three years who have taught me at least as much as I've taught them; my publisher Nancy Bereano who was consistently enthusiastic about this work; and the Minnesota State Arts Board whose support made it possible for me to complete the manuscript.

To my youngest brother and his fiancée—thanks for being so supportive when I told you about the book. To the rest of my family—I hope you take this writing in the spirit of healing and reconciliation with which it is intended. To William Butler Yeats—the second coming you divined and so feared, and the subsequent cracking open of civilization as we've known it, begins again each time one of the marginalized voices of the twentieth century breaks form and, our time come around at last, tells the truth.

to Mary Kay

contents

slouching towards chicago   11

a body's documentary   35

the opposite of god   49

the kiss   81

burning down the house   101

miss south side of chicago   119

restoring the color of roses   143

Turning and turning in the widening gyre
The falcon cannot hear the falconer;
Things fall apart; the centre cannot hold;
Mere anarchy is loosed upon the world. . .
. . . And what rough beast, its hour come round at last,
Slouches towards Bethlehem to be born?

"The Second Coming," W.B. Yeats

slouching
towards chicago

1.

I used to think you had no feeling," one of my closest friends said to me. "Now I see; it's just that you're from Chicago."

This was Minneapolis, and I was celebrating the first anniversary of my sobriety. My friends, the ones who had stayed with me through the changes, hugged me, handed me cards and wrapped packages. My lover, Linnea, kissed me on the cheek, whispered in my ear, "I still love you. I still love us."

I grew up a few blocks south of Chicago, at the edge of a horseshoe of suburbs that cluster the city's southern industrial base. This is the Calumet region on the far South Side, named for the Calumet and Little Calumet Rivers, dirty ribbons of water that cut though a plain of steel mills and paint factories, then run south into the suburbs.

Riding Amtrak into Chicago from the south, the train passes ✗ through the Calumet region. Wisconsin Steel, Sherwin-Williams Paint, the dead Little Calumet River. Slag heaps, piles of deflated car frames, unsteady jumbles of splintered railroad ties, crumpled barrels, cracked pieces of wall, bent wheels, cement chunks, crushed light bulbs, ceramic shards.

And paper, oh the paper. Newspapers, hamburger wrappers, flyers, shopping bags. Greasy and wadded, or flat sheets rising in the smoking air.

Closer in, through the South Loop, the warehouses are abandoned, windows punched out, gray-streaked walls marked with
gang insignias and AmeriKKKa in six-foot-tall graffiti.

I come from the edge of all this. The outer south edge of the
city. The lower edge of the middle class. The Polack edge of
white. Just over the edge of black South Chicago. A bit of an edge
on black south suburbia. I come from the inside lip of alcohol.
I am the lesbian edge of my family.

All my relatives come from Chicago: Eastern Europe to the
Minnesota Iron Range and then down into Chicago. South Side.
Catholic. Democrat. White. Croatian. German. Polack. Pronounce it Chi-*caw*-go. If you're white and don't pronounce the
long *aw*, the Mayor Daley drawl, you are not from there. Sometimes in Minneapolis I'll look out over some bank of the Mississippi River and notice a few faceless silos, one or two smoking
pipes, a sliver of what I know of urban industry, and Chicago's
South Side will tug at my gut. I come from some place ugly, and
I miss it.

2.

It's been more than ten years since I've lived in Chicago.

When I visit without Linnea I travel by plane. Flying into
Midway alone I am always afraid. The flight from Minneapolis
is only fifty-five minutes. The plane begins its descent just a few
minutes after reaching its highest point. This is too fast to get
back to Chicago. I see Lake Michigan, the John Hancock, the
smoke of the mills, and my stomach twists.

The white women in the airport all look like my Aunt
Cecilia—the prominent Eastern European nose, frosted hair ratted just a bit at the crown, wearing low-heeled pumps with

slacks on a Saturday. My brother Paulie is late picking me up, so I sit.

I think of my cousin Antony, the Italian, Cecilia's son, sitting in front of the television watching Al Jarreau sing on a variety show. "That *nigger*," he says, in a half-whisper, "that *fag*."

I think of Grandpa Luschak who was always drunk, who always looked dead, his eyes without focus, his skin without color.

I think of my mother the first time I brought my lesbian friends home to meet her. She scurried around my old bedroom wearing red earmuffs and wielding scissors, cutting off the protective plastic that had covered the dresser lamp for ten years, while she pretended not to notice which of these women set her sleeping bag down next to mine.

It's always like this, returning to Chicago, to the South Side. The images race through me like fast snatches of videotape.

Paulie drives up and I wonder if I have really changed. It is my greatest hope that I have. Perhaps I have changed so much that I will tell my little brother, tell him that I love it here, I love even this dingy airport, yet I am so scared when I'm in Chicago. I'll tell him how hard it is for me to talk to Mom. I'll tell him how Grandpa rose from the dead in me and how I sent him away.

Paulie jumps out of his black sports car and grabs my suitcase. "Hi, how you doin'," he says. It's not really a question.

"Fine, I am fine," I say, and I know that again, this time, I will show no feeling.

3.

When I visit Chicago with Linnea, we drive down in her truck, eight hours of freeway to prepare.

After dinner with my family, Linnea and I volunteer to drive Grandma Luschak home. To get to Grandma's from the south suburbs we exit the Calumet Expressway at Stoney Island. Cresting the hill just off the exit, the car seems to hover a moment. On all sides the land is charred and gray. It looks like a nuclear graveyard, framed with a ring of smoke-bellowing factories. The air stinks of sulfur dioxide. The smell stirs me, brings back memories of Grandpa Luschak.

Grandma lives in the same neighborhood she's lived in since she had my mom, her first child. South Dearing on the far South Side. The projects where Mom grew up are only two blocks away from the apartment where Grandma lives today. "I only pay a hundred dollars a month, see," she tells us today. "As long as old John downstairs stays alive I'll only have to pay a hundred a month."

All the billboards on this street show black people drinking bourbon or smoking cigarettes. On the drive down the hill my grandma asks me if I still drink.

"No, Grandma, I don't drink at all." She asks me this every time we talk. She doesn't say why, but I'm sure it's because she saw me drunk at least once, throwing up on the front lawn of my Aunt Lucy's house at my parents' twenty-fifth anniversary party.

At the bottom of the hill is a row of yellow brick apartments. All the people on the street here are black. "It's turned all Black around here," Grandma whispers. "It used to be just Mexicans, but now it's Blacks."

"Well, good thing Grandpa's not around anymore," I say, not wanting to agree with her. Not wanting to fight with her. "I sure would hate to hear him complaining about that."

"Oh yes, he sure would complain," and she laughs. A dry chuckle.

"Grandma," I say—I want to change the subject, but I also want information—"what was it like living with Grandpa?"

"Oh, it was hard," she says. She knows I am talking about

Grandpa's drinking. She looks away, out the window, her head nodding slightly. "I thought about leaving, but I had four kids. How would I live? I never had no job."

I look at Linnea, who is driving. We widen our eyes at each other. It's so unusual for anyone in my family to admit that anything has been hard.

"Grandma, my father is a drunk," Linnea says. "My mother used to say the same thing. 'I have four kids, how can I leave?'"

"Your father?" Grandma asks.

"Oh yes," Linnea says.

"Ohhh, then you know," Grandma says.

"Did Grandpa ever try to stop?" I ask.

"Oh, he went to the A and A. His boss at work made him go. But he always bought a bottle on the way home. I went to the one for the wives, but I didn't like it. It was just a bunch of ladies complaining. I didn't see no purpose to it."

The A and A. That made it sound like a root beer stand. I force myself not to laugh, and when I look over at Linnea again I see she is biting her bottom lip.

"Was Grandpa a drinker when you met him?" I ask.

"Oh no, that didn't start until later, see. He took this extra job at night, in the projects, driving a local politician around. They were supposed to pay him but instead they gave him free liquor."

We pull up in front of Grandma's building. "This block looks real good," I say. "All the houses are still in good shape."

"Do you have Blacks in Minnesota?" she asks me as I walk her to her door. I glance back at the truck. Linnea is waving.

"Look, Grandma, Linnea is waving good-bye."

"She's a nice girl," Grandma says, waving back at her. I can't tell if she knows who Linnea is to me.

"Do you have Blacks there?" she repeats.

She asks me this every time I visit Chicago. I dread this question, and yet I welcome it. In Minnesota I surround myself with a new family, the ones who are like me, outsiders, exiles from other places, other families. Among them I'm rarely forced to take a stand.

"Of course, Grandma," I say. "Of course there's black people. I like living around lots of different people, all mixed together."

"Ohhh," she says, but she looks puzzled. I kiss her dry cheek and open the front door.

4.

In Minnesota I dream of the South Side of Chicago.

I dream I am with a woman named Kip, sitting at a bus stop in South Dearing, Mom's old neighborhood. My mother is a few blocks away, with her friends, swimming in the Trumbull Park pool. When we left she was wearing a yellow one-piece bathing suit with padded cups and a bumpy yellow bathing cap with a rubbery pink flower over her left ear. I notice she is still a girl, too young to be my mother. Her thighs are thick, like mine, but her feet look tiny, too tiny to hold her. Kip nudges me and says, "Let's get out of here."

Kip and I stare into each others' faces and keep repeating, "Where did I know you before?" I am afraid of Kip because she has a flask of vodka in the pocket of her jeans jacket, yet I love Kip for her narrow bird-face, her tiny white nose, her pale freckles. She gives me a cigarette, and as I inhale it all the way into my lungs, I chant to myself: *I am an addict, I am an addict, I am an addict.* I know if I stay with her I will drink some of her vodka.

Kip stubs out her cigarette and says to me, "I hate this neighborhood. Too many niggers."

"*Niggers, niggers!*" I scream it back into her face. "You can't say that," I say. "That's not OK to say."

"*Niggers*," she repeats drily, and lights another cigarette.

In this dream I jump to my feet. "Listen," I say, "I'm a lesbian. So what do you think of that?"

I think of my mother in her padded yellow suit, lying flat on the surface of the water, arching her back, gliding into a water ballet trick, a back dolphin, submerging the pink-flowered cap, her body a circle underwater, then the yellow cap breaking through the water's surface, leading her body up into the sun. I will return to Trumbull Park and watch my mother swim. I turn around, stomp away from Kip, and just then I realize I'm out on the street, on the South Side of Chicago, wearing nothing on my feet but slippers.

"Oh yeah," Kip screams after me, "look at those Polack shoes."

5.

My mother's chin stiffens when TV comedians play drunk.

It was common when I was a kid. Goofy, slack-lipped, rubber-kneed comics stumbled across the stage of the Ed Sullivan or Dean Martin show, right after Sammy Davis, Jr. danced, or Tony Bennett sang. I remember one in particular, dressed in a black suit, his hair and beard salt-and-pepper, his belly round. He stumbled to his knees and swayed, slurring, "Exthuse me Ma'am, can I thake your goat?" and the audience roared.

"That's not funny," my mother murmured. I didn't have to ask her why. I knew it reminded her of Grandpa. She never said more. No one did.

Until the time Paulie brought it up during a long-distance call from Chicago. "Did you know Grandpa used to go to the track?"

"Really? I thought he spent all his money on booze."

"No, I guess he blew a lot of it on horses."

"How do you know?"

"Since I've been living at home, I get stuck picking up Grandma all the time."

"It must've been really hard for her," I said, "living with him."

"But don't you think it was Grandma who drove him to drink? She's pretty irritating. I sure want to drink after I've been with her."

When he said that I realized what I already knew. We're supposed to think it's Grandma's fault that Grandpa was a drunk. Grandma is pure Polack. Of course it was her fault, and so, by association, my mother's fault. I know Paulie didn't think this up himself. In my family these myths grow underground until they spring from our mouths as absolutes. As facts. Part of me believed it, too. *It's Grandma's fault that Grandpa drank.* That's what we've always said about it, when we've said anything at all.

"I don't think Grandma's irritating," I said.

"Huh, you're in Minnesota. You don't have to be her chauffeur."

"Paulie, you can't make another person a drunk." I said this righteously. This was before I went to treatment for drinking, one of the times I was white-knuckle dry and feeling superior about my sacrifice.

I felt him tune out. "Yeah, whatever," he said. Paulie was grown, graduated from college, about to go to law school. Still, he's the baby and I'm the big sister. Paulie tries to be on my side, but sometimes I push him too far, try to make him choose me over the others. There wasn't much more to say so we hung up.

Later I wondered how this version of the story had started. When did Grandma Luschak begin getting the blame? When we were kids my half-Italian cousins, the ones from my father's side of the family, called her Grandma Poo-Poo. It was probably because Grandpa Luschak worked for the Sanitary District, or maybe because she was Polish, or maybe just because her wig was too obvious. "I got a cold, see. I didn't wash my hair, so I got my wig on," she'd say holidays.

I never saw where they lived in the projects, but I'd heard my mom talking about it. "It was so dirty there," Mom said. "My mother's a terrible housekeeper. On Saturday afternoons before I had dates I used to scrub the walls until my hands were red."

The first time Linnea came with me to visit my family she found herself alone in the kitchen with my mother. My mother is not quite comfortable with Linnea, her daughter's spouse, this odd son-in-law who is a woman. My mother can't say *lesbian*. It's worse than *Polack*, a bad word like *nigger*, unmentionable, like saying Grandpa was a drunk.

"She started talking like I wasn't even in the room," Linnea told me later. "She said she had a dog she loved when she was a little girl. She said her father used to beat it."

"I didn't know what to say," Linnea told me. "She wasn't looking at me when she said it. I didn't say anything, and after a few minutes of quiet she stared me straight in the face and asked, 'So, are you a Minnesota Vikings fan?' "

6.

The night before I move away from Chicago I go out to dinner with Mom. The Sibley Boulevard Red Lobster is like any chain fish restaurant in the Calumet suburbs—$5.98 seafood specials and waitresses from Thornridge High, perky white girls in gold hoop earrings and lip gloss. I'm here with my mother because she asked me to come. She never wants to be alone with me, so I don't get what's going on. *It's nineteen-fucking-eighty for Godsakes! She waits until I'm twenty-one-years old to try to be my buddy?* The waitress brings us both plates of Shrimp Olé.

A lot of the customers in the Red Lobster tonight are black. It used to be you saw mostly whites in the mile this side of Halsted, but these days you see almost as many Blacks. I'd hear stories just a few years back when I was in high school: Blacks move onto an all-white cul-de-sac and some crazy whites spray-paint swear words on their garage door. Now you have to go a few blocks farther south to find streets where only white people live. But the waitresses here are still all white girls—the too-blond, smiley kind that I hope are nothing like me.

Mom doesn't know me very well. For instance, I've already had a woman lover, but Mom never met her. She's only met my kind-of-boyfriend, Leonard, and she thinks he's weird because he wears a beard and is still a student at thirty-three. Leonard just moved away from Illinois to buy a house in Minneapolis with his best friend BJ. Now I'm moving, too. To meet woman lovers? To be near him? I'm not sure. I don't have a job, only a little money, and last month I had a major operation. They cut into me, just above my pubes, a bikini cut the doctor said. I lost an ovary and a big old cyst the size of a balled-up fist. I'm thinking, when I get to Minneapolis I might get a job in a bar.

"It's awfully funny, two men buying a house together," Mom says to me.

"What's so funny?" I know what she's getting at, but I refuse to make it easy for her if she's not going to be direct. There's a big Bears game tonight, and some of the people around us have portable TV's. A man at a nearby table shouts and raises two fists in the air.

"Do you think you and Leonard will get married?" She doesn't sound hopeful.

"No, Ma."

She's pale, possessed by a mood I can't identify. I can't think of another time, ever, that she's asked me questions about my-self. "This women's liberation, you can take it too far," she says. My shrimp tastes like sand. I got drunk last night on blackberry brandy, and my head still throbs.

"What's *too far*, Ma? I don't take it too far."

"I just don't think unfairness toward women is as important as other things." She looks around the restaurant. "Like preju-dice against black people. That's more important."

She's surprising me. Mom never likes to talk about things in the world. Usually it's my dad who wants to talk current events.

"I'm against racism, Ma," I say, "but other things are impor-tant, too." Her jaw is so stiff. She doesn't want to hear what I think about it.

"But would you ever. . . ," and she stops for a minute. She takes a breath before she talks again. "Would you ever do. . . things. . .with women?"

Oh no, what was this? My hangover is expanding. The room is stretching all out of shape. The mini-TV's at the tables around us look like eyes. I never expected her to ask me this. I can't think of anything to say except yes.

And now the implications are clear. Not only will I *do* it, I will *be* it. And this is what I didn't get before. People are going to hate me for this.

Mom's face crumbles. We both push our plates to the cen-ter of the table. The room is trembling. My mother is crying. The Bears make a touchdown, and a hoot rolls over the dining room.

"Ma," I say, "you shouldn't ask questions if you don't want to hear the answers."

7.

We spend alternate Thanksgivings with my half-Italian cousins. We've done it this way since 1959, the year my cousin Antony and I were born. Now Antony and I are fifteen, and everything is the same as it's always been.

Aunt Cecilia, a Croatian, my father's sister, married an Italian bricklayer, and now she makes homemade *ravioli*. Italians know *lasagna, canelloni, manicotti, gnocchi, canolli, biscotti*. Italian is better because they have better food. My father buys special recipe books, Croatian cuisine—*cevapcici, raznici, sarma*. None of this is food he's tasted. Italians are better because they know their own food, but Croatians are better than Polacks. Polacks are good for nothing but *pirogi*.

My father follows a recipe from a bartender's handbook. Coffee, cream, whiskey. I think how funny Dad is, how good he is at jokes that you have to be smart to understand. He pours the heavy liquid into a slim brown bottle, tapes a hand-scrawled label to the front: Croatian Creme. It is a gift for his Italian in-laws. Italians are better than Croatians. Croatians are better than Polacks. We discuss this every holiday, the adults tipping back full glasses of wine, Antony and me slipping wine into our water glasses, all of us laughing and shouting across our full plates. My mother makes an occasional squeak, but we all wave our hands in her face, out-shout her. It's generally understood that my father, almost middle-class, married down when he married my mother, a Polack from the projects. Now her children are all Croatian, and every year we abandon her again. Polacks are the worst, except for the Blacks.

I know my father does not agree about the Blacks, but he won't argue with his relatives. Later he will tell me, ''These people have lived here all their lives. They don't know any better. It's not their fault that they're prejudiced.'' I am exactly like my father. That's what everyone tells me. And I do want to be just like him. I do want to be smart. My father teaches high school literature. He knows the words that will convince me to shut up. At dinner we all agree to let general consensus ride. Polacks are the worst, but thank God we're all better, at least, than the Blacks.

8.

Summers I tan deep brown, and my hair turns nearly white. This summer, just before fourth grade, my neighbor Marcia says, "You look like a *nigger*." She says it with spit in her voice.

Marcia is popular. She wears shiny flowered dresses with matching panties, and her legs are skinny. There's a crease in the middle of her right knee. I think she likes people to notice that crease in her knee because at school she sits sideways at her desk, her legs stretched out into the aisle. She caresses the crease with the middle finger of her hand.

I know we're supposed to say black people, not *nigger*. I know black people don't live in our neighborhood, Riverdale, because people like Marcia's father, the Captain of Police, have spit in their voice. I glare at Marcia, my meanest glare, but I am afraid to say anything to her. I am afraid she will say something bad about me to her friends and everyone in fourth grade will laugh at me.

Back in first grade I was still trying to be friends with Marcia. One day, at milk time, we lined up over black-and-white tiles through the Jefferson school gym room. The milk was in the refrigerator, individual-sized cartons. I was behind Marcia in line. I whispered to her, "If you step on a black tile you're black." She giggled. Still, I didn't enjoy it. I knew about Martin Luther King. My Dad even saw him once, near Mom's old neighborhood, in front of the Lion's Den—Grandma Luschak's favorite restaurant.

Martin Luther King was leading a whole march of black people down the middle of the road. They were mad because they weren't allowed to live in that neighborhood. I could tell by the way my Dad talked about it that it was an amazing thing to see, like a car crash or a house on fire.

We aren't allowed to say prejudiced things in my house, except about Polacks. My Italian cousins say *nigger*. Aunt Cecilia and Uncle Tony don't care. Grandpa Luschak hates black people. When he gets really drunk, he won't stop talking about how much he hates *niggers* and Mexicans. I guess he can't help what he says when he's drunk. I don't know why I said that thing to Marcia. I just looked down at those tiles and thought: black people/white people/black people/white people. It just popped out of my mouth, and Marcia giggled.

9.

Marcia has three P.O.W. bracelets. They're made of metal and have the names of soldiers engraved on them. My neighborhood, Riverdale, has its own Vietnam P.O.W. who was set free. His name is Sgt. Joe Osowski, and now he is standing on a platform that was built specially for him in front of the glass doors of the Riverdale police station and jail. He is skinny and he's dressed all in gray. His hair is stiff brown and stands straight up.

I've seen the Riverdale jail. Police Captain Cook gives a tour every year to the fourth grade. The cells are painted navy blue and the toilets are shiny white. There's never anyone in it, at least not during the tours. My uncle tells a story about the time my father went to jail. "Ben calls me up," tells Uncle Tony, "and he says, 'Come get me, I'm in the drunk tank.' The cop pulled him over for speeding, see, and Ben said he wasn't speeding, so the cop says give me your driver's license, and Ben says no, I wasn't speeding, so they throw him in the drunk tank. So I go over and get him from the drunk tank and it costs me fifty bucks.''

Everyone always laughs at this story, but I don't understand it. Was Grandpa Luschak ever in the drunk tank? Does the drunk tank look like the Riverdale jail? The jail where Sgt. Joe Osowski stayed in Vietnam must be how I imagine Purgatory: big, square warehouse rooms, like the ones with the popped-out windows you see from the train on the way downtown. The bodies are stacked on top of one another, like frozen chickens.

Sgt. Joe Osowski looks as if he's been frozen. He looks as if he isn't thawed out all the way, and I think that's how Grandpa Luschak looks too—like a man who isn't thawed out all the way. Sgt. Joe Osowski's legs move stiff, and so do his lips. There are about a hundred people at this rally, their round, peachy faces getting red in the chilly afternoon wind. Their signs bob up and down, and it looks like something from TV. Some people hold signs with Sgt. Joe Osowski's picture on it, or else with a picture of a blue star, like the ones people keep in their window if they have a son in Vietnam.

My mother drove me and Marcia down here, even though it's just eight blocks, close enough that we could have walked. Mom doesn't like me to walk too far in the neighborhood. ''Unsavory characters might be hiding in the weeds,'' she says.

My mother has teary eyes; I don't know why. She's never been to Vietnam. Maybe it's because she's Polish, like Sgt. Osowski. The people push in close while Sgt. Osowski talks with his frozen chicken lips, and Marcia runs off to where two other girls from school are standing. They are comparing P.O.W. bracelets. They look a lot like the I.D. bracelet that turned Katy Kaminski's wrist green. She's a few years ahead of me in school, but everyone knows who she is because she got that bracelet from a black guy. He's her boyfriend. She refuses to take the bracelet off even though she had to have a special meeting about it with the school nurse. She really looks like a Polack with that green ring around her wrist. I wonder if they have a special jail for Polacks in Vietnam. I wonder if all the Polacks are frozen like chickens until the bracelet on some Polack girl's wrist turns green—then they get to come home and have a rally.

Mom drives the long way home past Ivanhoe Park, by the commuter tracks. In my head I keep seeing a room full of frozen Sgt. Joe Osowskis stacked up, hunks of frosty ice with skin showing through. Then, in the street in front of the station wagon, I see a flapping chicken. I squeal and grab my mother's arm. She hits the brake and swerves. A big piece of cardboard rolls by in front of our radiator grill, over the curb, up onto someone's front lawn.

"I thought it was a chicken," I said.

Mom's lips are tight over her teeth. She narrows her eyes at me and pulls back onto the road.

"That doesn't look like a chicken, you stupid," Marcia says, poking me in the neck from the back seat, her P.O.W. bracelet rattling in my ear. "Anyway, chickens don't live in Chicago."

I close my eyes and see myself laid out in a freezer. God uses big black tongs to drop my frozen hunk on top of my mother's.

10.

My dad built a wet bar in the basement. Christmas, that's where Grandpa sits.

The Christmas tree is in the basement too, and the long table where we eat Christmas dinner. Christmas is just my mom's relatives: Grandma Luschak and Grandpa; my Uncle Francis and Uncle Luke, Mom's brothers; and the twin sisters they married, Aunt Theresa and Aunt Margaret Mary, who both used to be nuns. My mom's sister, Aunt Lucy, is there too, with her husband,

Uncle Joe—who makes good money selling industrial plastic bags—and her three little boys, my cousins.

My aunts and uncles sit around the tree and sip cocktails my father makes for them at his bar. I don't sit with them. I can never think of what to say. I sit in a beanbag chair between them and the bar, petting the dog, listening to my Aunt Margaret Mary talk about one of the girls she works with downtown at Exchange National Bank.

"The girl just went off and got married one weekend, didn't tell a soul. On Monday she walks in and says 'Change my nameplate. I'm married now.' Can you believe it? Just like that. *Change my nameplate.* I think there must be a reason. None of us have seen her husband. I'll just bet he's a colored man." She whispers when she says the word *colored.*

I hear my mother upstairs, arguing with my grandmother about a Jello mold. My brothers and my cousins are playing war with knives and forks from the dinner table I set before everyone got here. Grandpa sits at the bar drinking whiskey after whiskey.

I go up to the bar to get a maraschino cherry for my 7UP. I'm just twelve, not allowed to have liquor, but I like the idea of drinking something that looks like a cocktail. If I pour a little cherry juice in, and pop a cherry on top, I can sit by myself in the beanbag chair until dinner, imagine I'll have a job in a big office building downtown, have streaked hair like Aunt Lucy, and a narrow skirt and hosiery. After work I'll go alone to a dark bar on the first floor of my office building to drink a cocktail. Then I'll take a cab to my apartment at the very tip-top of a downtown skyscraper where I can drink fancy wine in skinny stemmed glasses and stare out at the city lights completely alone until morning.

Once Grandpa's really drunk, I try to stay away from him, but this time I forget. I just need that maraschino cherry. As I lean over the bar he grabs my shoulder, pulls me onto his lap.

"Bebe, come here by Daddy." Oh no, not again. Bebe is my mother's name. He holds me tightly by the shoulders, jogs me up and down on his knee. The knee pokes between my legs, all the way up, so I feel it pressing against my underwear. "Horsey, Horsey," he whispers in his bleary voice. I want to cry, but then someone might notice. I'm not a baby. I'm not Bebe.

I wrench away from him. His fingers are cold and weak. I fall to the ground on my knees. "Whattsa matter, Bebe?" he says. I don't answer. I stand up and brush myself off. It's important that nobody notices me. "Come here, Bebe. Come here," he's saying, but he's not looking at me. He's looking into his whiskey glass, mumbling my mother's name. I run upstairs, lock myself in the bathroom, sit on the edge of the sink, and look at my face in the mirror. Do I look like my mother? I feel trembly and not at all hungry for Christmas turkey.

11.

When I am eighteen, the year Grandpa Luschak dies, I discover that gin and tonics make family holidays fun.

I work in a supper club and know how to make drinks, so I take over my dad's post behind the bar—mixing martinis and old-fashioneds, and sipping gin and tonics with floating triangles of lime. If anyone knows I am drunk, they don't say. I think they are delighted that finally Barrie, that solemn girl who used to slouch around the corners of the party, sits among them, laughs at their jokes.

The holidays have changed. After Grandpa died the rules no longer applied. Here it is Thanksgiving, my mother's turn to cook, and both sides of the family have come, clustered around the bar in the basement of my parents' house. The Italian cousins. A Croatian great-uncle. My dad's mom, Grandma Rose, the regal Bohemian. My mom and her mother, the Polacks.

At the dinner table Grandma Rose announces that she wants great-grandchildren. "Which one of you will give me my first great-grandchild?" she asks, sweeping her hand across the table, letting her open palm rest for a moment before both my brothers, each of my cousins, and then me.

"We'll get you a *nigger* baby, Grandma," my cousin Antony says, and his little brother laughs.

"Oh no, no black babies," Grandma Rose says.

I sip my gin and tonic, suck on a lime. I see words fall around me in green shimmering waves. Grandma doesn't want any black babies. I think, I'll show them. I'll have a black baby just to show them.

"Barrie doesn't want babies," my mother says. "She's a women's libber."

"Oh, Mom," I protest. "*Women's libber?* No one says women's libber."

"Maybe Barrie should be a nun?" Grandma Luschak suggests. "If she doesn't want to get married . . . nuns don't get married."

My mother laughs. "She's no nun. She's a philanthrope."

"What?" I spit my lime back into my drink. I am nearly screeching. "A philanthrope? What does that mean, Mom? That doesn't make sense."

"I think that's Polish for misanthrope," my father says, laughing. "That's the Polack way to say you're a man-hater."

"*Philanthrope, misanthrope,* you know what I mean," Mom says. Everyone is laughing. Even my mother is laughing. She's always known how to take a good Polack joke. I am laughing the loudest of all. I am laughing so hard the room is a swirling green mirror of my family's grinning faces. I suck on my lime, sip my gin and tonic. She is not my mother, I think. I have no mother.

12.

In the first three months after my last drinking relapse I dream about drinking every night.

In one of these dreams I see my mother. We are at a big Chicago wedding, somewhere on the South Side. I'm drinking from a giant bottle of white wine, a bottle as big as the length of my arm. I hold the bottle over my open mouth, let the wine roll down my throat. Immediately I feel my skin dissolve. Grandpa stirs alive in me, and I guzzle.

I see my mother watching me and I panic. *I can't let her see me drink. I can't let her know I'm like Grandpa.* I run from the reception, lugging the heavy bottle. She runs after me. Outside, on an industrial road strewn with heaps of rusted iron slag, I trip. The wine spills, mixes with rust-colored dirt, streaking orange mud over the front of my dress.

When my mother catches up to me in this dream, I say, "I'm worse than a Polack. Worse than a lesbian. Mom, I'm like Grandpa."

She brushes the mud off my dress. Her bare hands turn orange. When she speaks she has spit in her voice. "How could you show up at a wedding in a dress like that. I'm so embarrassed for you."

13.

My father stands before a glob of metal embracing itself.

We are in Minneapolis at the Walker Art Center sculpture garden. My parents are visiting me from Chicago. We've just come back from brunch at the top of the IDS building in downtown Minneapolis—my parents, Linnea, and I. This is the first time my parents have visited since I've lived with a woman lover.

At brunch my father had ignored me. He talked to Linnea in a low, slow voice, telling her about interesting people he'd noticed on his early morning jog through downtown Minneapolis. "But where are all the black people here?" he asked her. "This restaurant, for instance. There's not one black person here."

We could see out over the city though the blue glass walls that circled the restaurant. The green and copper of autumn trees, the flat green mirrors of the city lakes, the long brown snake of the Mississippi.

"There's a black man, by the window," my mother offered. "Look, he's with a white woman. Do you think they're married?"

"God, Mom, don't point," I said.

My dad looked up at us, his lips pursed. Now I understood, he was trying to engage Linnea in an intellectual discussion about black people, or Minneapolis landmarks, or anything to keep his mind off the fact that the woman he was sitting across from was his daughter's lover. My mother and I were distracting him.

I remembered what he said several years before when I came out to him. "Dad, disliking this about me is like disliking that I have green eyes, or that I'm tall. It's just a thing about me."

"Yes," he'd said. "I understand that is one of the theories."

We were on long distance when he said it, so I couldn't see his face. But I imagined he looked as he did at that restaurant table, his lips pinched, his eyes half-lidded and dull. I wondered if the inside of his mouth was as bitter as the look on his face. Could he even taste his expensive breakfast?

His discussion with Linnea was over. I don't know if it was Dad's expression, or just some flicker in my mother's mind that started it, but all at once, quick-fire, my parents were arguing.

"Minneapolis is the only major city with a Big Ten team," my mother announced. It was meant as a challenge.

"Well, what about Northwestern, Bebe."

"Northwestern's not really in Chicago. It's in Evanston." My mother's face was hard-set. The fight continued through the remainder of the meal.

In Linnea's truck, after brunch, on our way to meet my parents at the sculpture garden, a song came on the radio. *It's gonna take an ocean of calamine lotion. . . .* "I hate this song," I said.

Linnea turned it up. When she started humming along I said, "OK, you're irritated with me."

"Can I just drop you off? It's not you. I just can't listen to another argument about the Big Ten."

And so I'm alone at the sculpture garden with my parents.

"I looked at this and thought, what on earth?" my father says to me. "I asked myself, is this mother and child? Then I looked at the marker." He laughs. "Look, it says *Mother and Child.*"

My father is proud to have cracked the mystery of the sculpture glob. Yes, this is my father, I think. My tall Croatian father. People used to say, "Your father is so handsome. He looks like Joe Namath." Dad's hair is white now. But he talks the same as he always has. He pauses first, contemplating, then when he speaks he does it slowly, carefully pronouncing each thoughtful word. He shows me no feeling, but he likes to think. I get it from him, this desire to think.

When I think of Croatia, I hear singing. High Balkan voices. I imagine Yugoslavian children standing, white-lit, on the hilltop in Medjugorje, entranced by a translucent, whispering, blue-robed Our Lady. *O Mother mine, Mother of goodness, love and mercy, I love you infinitely and I offer myself to you.* From my father I get the desire to believe I come from some place beautiful.

The three of us walk to the base of several giant metal sculptures. Rusted. Copper-colored. Obelisks, my father and I decide. Like Stonehenge, we agree.

My mother says, "This looks like a pile of slag from Wisconsin Steel."

My father sighs and walks away from her, but I do not. I

stand by her. I laugh. Yes, I have to admit, that is what it looks like. I can almost smell Chicago's South Side—industrial sulphur, gray soot whirling out of the smokestacks into the air, into my lungs.

My God, she is in me too. How could this be? I am from this tiny, frowning woman who holds her chin so tight it seems it might crack off? We move from the slag piles to a mesh dome with tiny articles attached to the inside wires. Chairs. Faces. Mathematical equations. Too much to look at all at once. A Chaos. "It looks like the Universe," my mother says.

I have to admit, at least for a moment, in this world I see more of slag heaps than Stonehenge.

"Yes," I say. "It looks exactly like the Universe."

a body's documentary

Tall as a Wall

When I was a girl I was so tall I had to stand with the boys in the back row of classroom photos. *Tall, tall, big as a wall.* But in first grade, the best thing to be was cute. The back row was embarrassing. In the back row I loomed, enormous and loathful, certain I was too tall, too fat, too odd. I wondered, *Am I really a girl?*

"We pronounce our last name Bor*ick*—like icky," Mom said. Dad's brother called us Bor*ich*, loving the spongy *ch* sound. "It got changed when our dad came over on the boat," Uncle Paul explained.

My father disagreed. "In Croatia it's spelled Boric. That means we're right to pronounce the *ick*."

I hated this name with icky inside it. I whispered it when I was alone, pronounced it Bor*ich* too. But even armed with my secret *ch*, nothing could make me a regular girl. *I don't want her, you can have her, she's too fat for me.* Too fat. Too tall. Too odd. *Hey, you, icky girl—your mother is a Polack.*

My class photos were stored in a sheer paper sleeve in a jumbled drawer with receipts, insurance policies, and leftover Christmas cards. I was in first grade, and my teacher frowned afternoons when I moved my seat back by the sink because some-

thing hurt, maybe my stomach. Maybe I would throw up. My report card said, *She is often ill.* The word *ill* sounded icky to me,
icky like the picture I saw in my head when Dad sang the "Too
Fat For Me Polka," the fat girl's flesh wobbling while she danced
stupidly. *You're too fat, you're too fat, you're too fat for me.*

I Could Not Do Cartwheels

Marcia could do cartwheels, and she did. Up and back across
the three lawns between her house and mine. The neighbors ap-
plauded. Marcia was cute and would grow into a cheerleader.

"Now you do it," the neighbors called to me. Marcia could
toss her hips over her head, steady as a wheel. I tried to balance
on the skinny support of my hands but could not bear to be up-
side down. Fear cupped the base of my brain, a wall between
what I could and could not be. In the privacy of my own yard
I tried to break through the barrier, kick my feet into the unstable
air, and feel the blood speed to my cheeks. Always the NO
responded, froze my joints. I would not.

Mom demanded I take ballet, in the back room of a neighborhood music store. I didn't want to dance, but she insisted.
Her only daughter could be different from her, thinner, more
ethereal, a dancer. She was just trying to save me from fat thighs,
the curse, she often told me, of all the women in her family.

I loved to gaze at Grandma's wedding photo, the only thing
beautiful I ever saw of her life. The photo was taken in the twenties. It looked like a black-and-white movie still, elegant and deco
moderne.

"Grandma was so beautiful."

"No, Grandma would have been beautiful if it weren't for
her thighs."

Plié. Relevé. I would have liked to have been good enough

for toe shoes, but I could not practice. I made charts, promised myself a silver star for every hour in motion, but I could not do it. Every Wednesday at 4:00 P.M. I went to the tiny backroom studio, and the teacher, Miss Carla, in her soft pink tights and leotard said, "No, no, that's not it. Hold your hands softer, like you're holding a goose egg." Each week I was no better. I did not like to feel my muscles stretching. I did not like to feel my body at all. It reminded me of ickiness, the wrong thing in me I had no name for. So I practiced ways to escape it. I lay on my bed and read novels, or stared up, silently, watching the airborne dust sparkle.

And so Mom failed. I did not plié away my peasant thighs. And I could never do cartwheels.

Marcia zipped past with the authority granted her by her cuteness and her father's status as police captain in our neighborhood of steelworkers, schoolteachers, and aging women in curio-shop houses. "Now you try it."

Why don't you ask me about a book? Can't you see I'm a smart girl, a smart girl? "You do it, you do it now." The neighbors teetered forward on their flimsy lawn chairs, cheering me on. *Oh, but I spit in your eyes, because cartwheels are stupid and Marcia gets* C's.

A Croatian Nose

My teacher, Miss Delich, was a Croatian, but she was lucky. She didn't have the nose. The night before fourth-grade class photos I asked Mom to cut the front of my long hair into bangs. I wanted to hide my face. Too long, I thought, too wide. I imagined it loomed out of my neck, led by the Croatian nose, a ship rocking into port. Croatian noses are handsome on men, but on girls, tragic. The nose was an inheritance from my dad, and one of the bombs my mother lobbed in the Croatian-Polack wars.

"Look at her. She even looks like you," Mom said.

It was dinnertime and I refused to talk. I was sullen and slumped over my pork chops and peas, everything else drowned out, made ugly by a low, hard noise that was caught inside my body. What was there to talk about? Pork chops? I hated pork chops. My two little brothers, who poked each other with the silverware and made gross spitting sounds in the back of their throats? I hated my brothers, both of them, nearly identical in their matching crew cuts and football jerseys. I hated our dishes, their pictures of yellow daisies with brown stems. I hated the fan screwed into the window that could blow both inwards and out, and always had little cakes of dust stuck to its plastic grid. I hated the long counter that stuck out like a peninsula, separating the kitchen table from the stove and refrigerator. The counter had speckled linoleum and yellow shelves underneath. Dad kept that stupid paddle there, a joke gift from Uncle Tony, the Italian. It was wooden and painted bright red. On the front was a cartoon of a man bent over, his face screwed up in pain, ouch marks flying off his butt like red lightning bolts.

Once Dad got mad when Mom said, "Look at her. She never talks. She's exactly like you." He picked up that paddle and slammed it against the spotted counter. It broke in two, and Mom screamed. I watched, did not speak. Dad never did things like that. What would happen next? Would the walls fall in? The furnace explode? Nothing happened. We went back to eating dinner. The low drone in my body resumed. I have Poli-sausage thighs, just like my mom, I thought, but my dad and I have exactly the same nose.

On picture day I could not find an outfit that would make my body disappear, but in the back row, at least, my sausage thighs could hide. I could only pray my nose would shrink beneath the crown of my new bangs.

Miss Delich noticed my bangs right away. She held my chin

in her hand. Her fingertips were soft. I closed my eyes to feel them better. I never told anyone that I had dreams about Miss Delich, and other teachers too, especially Mrs. Krebbs, my second-grade teacher who had to leave because she got pregnant. Sometimes I dreamt that Miss Delich kissed me on the mouth when I was sleeping. For a minute that's what I thought Miss Delich was about to do when she tilted my face up toward hers. Instead she announced, "Why you look like a Barrie Booper!"

BOOOOOOPER. Now I see she meant to be sweet, but then it sounded ugly to me, a low horrible name, a noise like the moan of a nose-heavy ship. I heard it inside me always, but this was the first time anyone said it aloud. BOOOOOOPER. I was too ugly to kiss. I was icky for wanting a kiss. She kept calling me that for the rest of fourth grade. BOOOOOOPER. BOOOOOOOOOOOOOPER. *It's my Booperness that makes me so bad.*

I Cannot Think of What to Say

I have a photo of myself at age sixteen that proves I was skinny. I thought that I was fat, yet I can see in the picture that I wasn't, not at all. I stand on the beach in a striped bikini. I am athletic, slender.

This was the year I started the grapefruit diets. For ten days all my meals were balanced portions of meat and grapefruit. The grapefruit acid seemed to dissolve all the meat, and so I felt like I shed calories every time I peed. By the fifth day my pants were looser and I was a bitch, furious with hunger. By the tenth I was spotty, ecstatic, stoned out of my usual sadness.

When I was skinny I felt a warm spotlight shine on me always, and I couldn't help but be beautiful. Even Mom liked it. "You look pretty with your hair long and your face so nice and thin," she said.

When I was skinny I flirted with boys, and it worked. Boys
asked me out and girls leaned close to hear about it. I sat with
a girl, cross-legged on the ground, by the tracks behind school
where we went to smoke pot, and if I made the story especially
dramatic, she'd tremble a little. She might let one hand fall to
my thigh or even pinch me. The girls loved the story of Roberto
Valdez asking me to the prom.

"He grabbed my arm in the hall," I leaned close to tell them.
"When I was on the way to Algebra. He was wearing this cool
white gauze shirt with Mexican embroidery. He practically begged me to go."

But my powers were short-lived. I broke the grapefruit fast
on Kit Kat Bars and M&M's. I gained the weight back in a day,
and for this I heckled myself. *You're fat, oh you're fat, you're
ugly and fat. None of my stories are as good as I tell them. I'm
not the girl I pretend to be.* I jeered and wished I could pull the
fat off my thighs in jellied handfuls.

If I was fat when these boys came to my house, I could not
think of what to say to them. It's not like they were girls. Would
a boy be interested in how to use a sewing needle to separate
mascara-clumped eyelashes? Would they care to know that I
never wanted children, that I did not believe in God? I went with
the boys into their fathers' cars. If they had automatic transmis-
sion, I sat close so they could put one arm around my neck and
steer with the other. On my first date with Roberto Valdez he
pulled a pink party joint out of his shirt pocket, and I smoked
it gratefully, hoping the dope would loosen my voice. He drove
me up into the East Side, the far southeast edge of Chicago, near
where my grandparents lived. At Calumet Park he led me down
to the Lake Michigan shore. He put one arm around my waist,
pulled my arm around his waist. "Walk like this," he said, and
took a monster step, first to one side, then another. Beach glass
crunched under the black leather soles of his boots and I stum-

bled along, trying to keep up, but BOOOOOOPER, BOOOOOOPER rang through my ears, magnified by marijuana, and I could not do it. I could not share this funny walk that he had certainly walked before, with some skinny girl, some talky girl, some girl who knew how to be a girl.

"What's the matter with you," he asked, exasperated. "You're not acting normal."

When I got home from dates, I ate. Whole boxes of Apple Jacks. Ho Ho's. Ding Dongs. Maurice Lenell Chocolate-Chip Cookies. All the leftover coffee cake. Each mouthful took me higher and higher toward some buzz that seemed to be existence, until sound exploded and I began to fall. Falling I could feel the weight of my flesh and I hated it, all of it.

So one night I thought of throwing up. A brilliant idea. I thought I'd invented it. I could eat all I want but never get fat. I could always be a thin and lovely girl. Leaning over the toilet, I stuck my finger down my throat. I gagged and gagged, but all I could manage were dry heaves. I gagged and gagged until finally I stopped to mop the sweat off my face and saw the ring of broken blood vessels surrounding my eyes. Marked. I was marked. Was it permanent? I was trying to rub the spots away when the doorbell rang.

Through the security glass I saw Roberto leaning against the bell. I had to make him stop ringing, before my parents woke up, but how could I explain my poxy face?

When I opened the door, I could see he was stoned, more than usual. "Come out and drive with me," he said.

"I can't. It's too late." I tried to stand in the shadow, so he wouldn't see my eyes.

"Come on. You won't get in trouble. Your mama likes me." It was true. He stopped by one afternoon when I wasn't home, talked to Mom for a whole hour. Ever since, she called him Mr. Dreamy. What could they have talked about for a whole hour?

He reached in, pulled me toward him, but when the light hit my face he stopped. I could see he was looking at my eyes, so what could I do? I told him all of it, that I ate too many cookies, that I tried to throw up, that I was afraid of getting fat. I laughed when I said it, like it was some great joke.

He stood still for a moment, then he spoke. "You and me, we have nothing in common." We both laughed at that. What could be more obvious? He handed me a joint on his way back down the steps. When he left I went outside behind the garage to smoke, felt my skin dissolve into the chilly night. I was no one, I decided, and there was no one like me.

A Soft Target

The frame of the photo begins at my waist. My face looks soft in the smoke of the joint I'm smoking; my eyes are heavy-lidded, unfocused. My nipples show through my white tank top. My hair, streaked platinum by the sun, is strewn around me on the quilt where I rest my head, and my lips are pursed slightly, like I'm ready to let someone kiss me.

I shot this photo when I was twenty, with a view camera I borrowed from the university art department, a heavy, antique-looking machine on a tripod that stood as high as my chin. I tipped the lens down over the mattress on my floor, and I laid down under it, stretching one arm up out of the frame to trip the shutter. The photo was shot from a lover's perspective, a body about to lie down over my body, about to spread apart my knees and come in.

It was an assignment for Luther's class. He was an art photographer in his forties, known for sleeping with his women students. I had just begun to examine my face close in my bathroom mirror. *Is that a lesbian?* I had never kissed a woman, but I'd met women I wanted to kiss. It had occurred to me recently that this might be the reason I always felt so outside everything. There could be a place for me, something to belong to. Did I want to go there? I thought I had to choose: a pretty girl, or a dyke. I didn't want to commit to anything I couldn't get out of.

The day I brought my self-portrait to class was the day Luther started staring at me, and I wasn't sure how to take it. Did it mean I was beautiful? Did it mean I was a lesbian, that he could see it? Did it mean he had picked me out from the other girls—an easy lay, a soft target?

I was an easy lay then, mostly because I was so often drunk. I went to parties, got wasted, and my body loosened under its skin. If I could draw a man to me, then I won. I was beautiful. I never really intended to let them fuck me, but once I was drunk I couldn't tell what was happening. When I saw Luther staring at me from the front of the class, I knew what I was supposed to do. Even there, sober in mid-afternoon as the class mulled over photographs we'd taken—an empty playground swing in lined shadow, a naked woman bending over behind a birch tree, an old woman's swelling feet—Luther stared. I wondered if I should stare back, meet his eyes. Could I turn away from someone who liked my body?

My final project for the class was a series of photographs of my legs. In the first I'm wearing pantyhose and high-heeled red sandals. In my hand I hold a copy of *Cosmopolitan* magazine. In the next I set the magazine on fire and take off the red shoes. In the last photo the magazine burns on the floor, the flame peaking, black smoke curling off its tip, and I walk out of the frame, my legs and feet bare. The fire set off the smoke alarm, charred the corner of the wicker mat I used as a carpet in my basement apartment, but that part didn't make it into the picture.

When I brought the photographs to class, I stared at my legs, long and thin in the hose and red stilettos. Naked, my legs looked more square, more thick across the thighs. *Can I really walk away?*

Luther pulled me aside, said my photographs were so controversial that the class overlooked technical questions—exposure, contrast, depth of field. Would I come to his office so we could discuss these issues in private?

I waited until the last moment of the semester to decide. I ran into Luther one afternoon before class at the art building cafeteria, and he sat down next to me. He asked me questions. "Where are you from? Are you serious about photography?" One of his colleagues joined our table, a white-haired man who taught figure drawing. I could tell he assumed I was sleeping with Luther by the way his eyes focussed on my mouth when he reached over the table to shake my hand. On our way to class Luther said it again. "Come to my office."

In the end, I decided not to go. I looked into my bathroom mirror and said, "I think I am a lesbian," and I cried a little because I thought that now I would not be able to be beautiful.

And Luther, he gave me a *C*.

I Am Beautiful

I snapped a photo of Irena the morning after we slept together for the first time. She sat in a sunbeam, a large and beautiful woman in a burgundy sweater, her soft hands folded in her lap.

I was crazy for Irena's black eyes, her sweet enormous breasts, and the way she slept with her head over my racing heart. I kissed her in public. I wanted to walk with my arms always around her. I loved her and made love with her. This was the first time it had ever happened to me. Before then I thought people, straights or queers, who made out in public were idiotic. Why would anyone want to act that way? But I changed when I fell in love with Irena. We could get shot, two women kissing on the street, but I didn't care.

Irena said to me, as she passed me a joint, "I'm fat, but I know I'm beautiful." She was beautiful, I agreed. But to have the nerve to say it, my God, that impressed me.

"You are beautiful," Irena told me when I lay naked with her on my futon, on the floor, in Minneapolis where we were safe, far from my mother who was still asking, "Have you gained weight?"

I stepped into my body, stretched into the muscles of my thighs. *My body is beautiful.* I felt my way up into my face. *My nose, my face is beautiful.* For a second I believed it.

I brought Irena home to Chicago for Christmas. I'd already come out to my mother, but she pretended to have forgotten. She knew I was with women, must have known Irena was my lover. I wasn't going to mention it until she brought it up. At the end of our stay my mother pulled me into the kitchen, poured us both a glass of wine. "I want to talk to you about your friend."

"She's fat," Mom said. "I'm afraid you think it's OK to get that fat."

I walked away, refused to listen. She was even worse than when I was a kid, a fanatic about physical fitness. To her being fat was worse than having cancer. I expected this from her, but suspected more, that there were words she wouldn't say. I suspected she meant, *I'm afraid. I don't want you to be a lesbian.*

I kept loving Irena, resisted my mother, but still I heard her voice for weeks. *Don't do that. You can't do that and be pretty.*

My Body's Hunger for Itself

I got skinny. I got so skinny my friends thought I might die.

I didn't mean to. It happened when I got sick. My body was rank with constant infection, my belly sliced open to remove a cyst the size of a softball. Later, I tried to explain it to my mom. We were looking at snapshots. I'm so skinny in one that my head, too large for my body, lobs to one side, a dying balloon.

"Look, you were so ultra-skinny, like a model."

"Ma, I was sick." *Can't she see?* "I was skinny because I had the shits for a year," I said. "I was starving to death."

"But it's nice you were so skinny." It hurt me to hear her say it.

I told her she was wrong, but did not admit that I missed being skinny, missed feeling my flesh settle so close to my bones. When I was skinny, I bought miniskirts, felt luminous and spectacular, free at last from my grandmother's thighs. When women who made love to me said, "You are beautiful," I believed them. I was lovely, a thin and lovely woman, and not just in the heated moments of love. I had to graze at the edge of my death to finally shut the Booper up.

"Maybe I should try that diet," my mother said. I think she was serious. My mother likes us both better half-dead, I thought.

"Ma, that's crazy. I don't want to be skinny." That's what I said, but I didn't believe it. When I got healthier my body fattened and I missed how it felt to be swinging on death's crooked arm, swinging and singing while my sad body gnawed away at itself.

I Don't Want to Be Skinny

When I stopped drinking and smoking dope, I began to remember my life. I hated what I remembered. Men who thrust their dicks in me even though I told them not to. It happened a lot. Remembering, I imagined. I wanted to fix it, to remember it better.

So I imagined myself with them, watching from above, my skin dead to feeling. Was I beautiful to those men? I imagined

I could have liked it if I tried, that their dicks were small and cautious as a finger, swelling up only when I wanted them to, imagined I could writhe and come and hold them shivering. I imagined it was turned around, that I was them, my dick pink and pulsing, pounding harder when I saw how young, how unstuck she was, and how I couldn't control it, had to, just had to keep pushing it in.

I imagined all this while I was working a switchboard, my head wired for sound in a too-bright room, answering calls for people who called me stupid. Outside was a drought, a solid wall of heat, and across the street a bar with a sign: GIRLS WANTED. The door was guarded by an old man chewing tobacco, his chair leaned unsteadily against the bricks. I'd seen the ads. *Girls wanted, make up to $600 a week.*

GIRLS WANTED. It beckoned to me. My body ached and I wanted to answer. I wanted to be a girl who wore garter belts, gave men erections for money.

I told my lover Linnea what I was thinking. She said, "Why would you want to do that?"

"I don't know, I don't know. I just feel like if I don't, I'll crack. I'll burst right open."

"I don't want men looking at you," she said.

I didn't either, not really. Still, I wondered why all those men from before wanted to have sex with me. *Am I a girl after all?* I wanted to know if they would still want to, if I was still pretty enough to give a man an erection.

"Those men you were with, they would have fucked anything. Why don't you believe me when I tell you you're beautiful?" Linnea's face was soft around her eyes. Sometimes she had so much trouble understanding me.

"But don't you think I'm fat, that my thighs are too fat? Don't you think I look bad in a bathing suit?"

She told me she wouldn't talk to me when I was talking

crazy. She said if I answered the ad she wouldn't stay.

On my way into work I avoided the stripper bar. I spent my breaks wandering the climate-controlled skyways, rewarding myself with treats, coffee that gave me headaches or breads that left me bloated. Finally, from my switchboard, I called the number in the ad, just to see who would answer, expecting a spittle-voiced man who would scare me out of it. But it was a woman, a secretary. It could have been me, except she was more polite. My switchboard buzzed with incoming calls and I hung up.

I didn't dial again the next time my board was quiet. Instead I picked up a catalogue from the break room, an advertisement for lingerie. For the first time I noticed how emaciated the models were, their D-cup breasts out of proportion to their skinny frames. Why hadn't I ever seen this before? I imagined one of those models crawling into my bed, and all at once I knew I would not like rubbing against their pokey knees, their sharp hips, would not like hugging their xylophone chests.

"I don't want to be skinny." I whispered it into their glossy, blank faces. "You're not the only ones who get to be girls."

I still wanted to answer the ad, but I knew now that I probably wouldn't. I rode home on the slow bus, and when I got there I drank a glass of mineral water with ice. I am ready, I thought, to stop this now.

At dusk I drove out to Cedar Lake to swim. My new swimsuit was two-piece, size twelve. I stood on the grassy beach, dropped my towel. Did I look too fat in my bathing suit? No one was here to look at me. I entered the lake, its water lukewarm from the drought. I dove under, opened my eyes. The water was golden with clay from the lake bottom, and I was golden too. I surfaced silently, and the water barely rippled. My body, the body of the lake—there was no separation between us. I floated, on my back, until the night sky darkened and I could see the first bright glint of stars.

the opposite of god

I'm standing here trembling on the Sibley Boulevard train platform, and it feels like the end of something. The air is sticky, even though it's early. Downtown, near Lake Michigan, it will be cooler. But here on the South Side, above the traffic, above the old cement buildings, the rows and rows of square brick houses, humidity sticks to everything like rubber cement.

It was breezy where Lilly lived, last time I saw her. But I don't mean to think of Lilly. I stand here in the thin 7:00 A.M. light on my way to the Chicago Loop, to my summer job as a clerk's assistant in the teller's circle of the Exchange National Bank, and without meaning to I keep thinking of throwing myself in front of the commuter train.

The urge to jump is a sound—high-pitched, almost a squeal, a kind of holy music filling me up as if it is me. I've just turned nineteen, finally legal in Chicago bars. In two weeks I return to college. I'm going to be a career woman, a journalist. There's no reason for me to think about something so stupid as jumping.

I can't blame Lilly for the music that keeps knocking around inside my body. It's just that all this is happening at once, the wanting to jump, the break between Lilly and me.

We made friends three years ago, in our high school journalism class. I was sixteen; she was a year older. We lived on opposite sides of Thornwood High in the first school district south of the Chicago line. My parents still live here, in South Holland, where our family moved just before I started high school. Technically, I guess, I still live here too, since I did come back from college for the summer. But I'm not staying. There's nothing but look-alike houses and perfect lawns and too many vacant, God-crazy people.

This suburb was founded by Dutch Reformed Lutherans, and they have this tulip thing: tulips painted on the garage doors, a tulip festival every spring where cutesy little blond girls dance around the streets in wooden shoes. But it's not just that. I swear there's a church on every other corner. I don't mean the Catholic kind where you can move through in a quick forty-five minutes, like a supermarket line, and then you're done for the week. The people that go to these Protestant churches all know each other, like they're related. They have JESUS SAVES bumper stickers and won't allow any bars or movie theaters within the town limits and the only place that's open on Sunday is Burger King.

There are Catholics here, too, mostly relocated from Stoney Island or the East Side, but we're not the main thing, not like my old neighborhood where I couldn't think of anyone who wasn't Catholic. Here, there's this Protestant haze over everything. Like the water tower—it has a picture of praying hands on it. Soft white hands, like you'd expect to see in a lotion commercial, except they have a slightly blue tinge to them. They hover over the freeway, these pale blue, floating hands, and I'm always half-expecting them to reach down and strangle me, which is part of the reason I have to get out of here.

Lilly's so heavy into God she could have been the original South Holland girl. But she spent her whole childhood a few blocks further south in Thornton, the suburb famous for its enormous stone quarry and great forest preserves perfect for partying. She lived with her mother and little brother in a big old wood house with screened-in porches and shutters, nothing like the dull split-level ranches in South Holland, and her yard bumped right up against the best party spot in the whole preserve. But Lilly didn't party back then.

Lilly, with her lank, cashew-colored hair, her square thighs, her invisible eyelashes—she's never been the prettiest girl around. She says she comes from a long line of Irish potato pickers, sturdy little people. Descended from elves, she says. But she has ways of acting that make people think she's a major fox. Not just me. When she isn't smiling, Lilly's face is plain, but when she smiles something happens. Her face opens up into a whole new scenery, a place I'd like to run into, roll around in. This isn't something I can actually see. It's more a feeling I get when she focuses on me. I mean, when she used to focus on me. That's in the past. I don't think I'll see her face again, except maybe on TV. She seems bound to be notorious, the kind of girl who will be involved in a sex scandal with a baseball player or a presidential candidate. At least that's what I expect.

There's always some guy crazy for Lilly. Back in high school, the smart guys who worked with her on the school paper would have done anything for her, but she wasn't interested. Lilly dated swim team boys, the ones with long muscles, shaved bodies, and bleached-out head hair that was limp and as silky as milkweed. She's always had a thing for blonds.

The main reason I started loving Lilly is that she's deep. I've always had a hard time finding friends to be deep with me. Most of the guys I've been out with are hopeless. My other girlfriends roll their eyes at me when I try to talk with them about ideas. *Do you believe in God? In marriage?* They roll their eyes, shrug at each other, pass the joint around the circle. *She's getting deep again.* They respect me for it; they just don't know what to say. These kids are great. I mean, I really love to party with them, but sometimes I think they have no future. They're smart enough, but they just don't know what they want to do with themselves. They never THINK about the WORLD.

Lilly's always answered any question I've asked her. "Do you believe in God?"

"Yeah. God's with me all the time, like my skin," she said, and she was serious. I didn't understand, but at least she answered me. She didn't ask me what I thought, but she didn't mind that I thought about things. And I envied her. She was so sure. She never seemed to doubt that there was a place scooped out for her in the world. I think she had some doubts, later, but when I first met her she seemed completely settled in.

It was gray and drizzling the day I started to love her. It was only two months before her high school graduation, and I'd already been worrying about what it would be like to be a senior with Lilly gone. That day, Lilly's coat was yellow and she was carrying an enormous yellow umbrella. I was standing in the school parking lot with some other girlfriends, the ones I partied with. They were all smoking cigarettes, but I don't smoke, except pot, so I was just hanging out with them before the first bell. Lilly walked by with that big yellow umbrella, and I worried that my friends would think she was a nerd. The wind whipped her coat up around her square knees. I could see the beige lace trim of her slip. Why does she wear a slip? I thought. Who wears a slip? Who would even wear a skirt to school? Lilly had no idea how to dress back then.

I wore jeans, or overalls with the straps unbuckled, and T-shirts with iron-on decals of my favorite bands—King Crimson or Procol Harum or Yes. *I've seen all good people turn their heads this way, so satisfied, I'm on my way.* I like the bands whose songs are like poems—words so great you could pray to them.

Most of the people I've partied with prefer Peter Frampton. *Wah-wah-wah-wah.* It creeps me out when he makes his guitar sound like it's talking. Or worse, they're into old Ted Nugent with all that stringy hair that I keep expecting to get caught in his guitar strings. Heavy metal has no poetry. Still, I don't know what kind of music Lilly likes best, which is so weird since it's usually the first thing I ask a person.

I groaned inside when I saw her that day. She looked so mainstream. But at the same time I felt her ON me in some strange way that I still don't understand. It was almost as if she was pressed up against me, as if I could feel her skin. Those square knees especially got to me. I couldn't stop looking at them. And all that yellow. She was the only thing in sight that had any color to it.

Lilly watched me over her shoulder when she passed, and then she smiled. Lots of people smile, but Lilly's smile was different. Other people's smiles have no meaning, no secret messages. Lilly's was a promise. We'll talk later, it said, and music rocked through me. *Lilly-la-lilly-lo-lilly-la-lilly-lo.* A Frampton guitar solo. Not my favorite, like I said, but familiar. Not me, but something that lived in me, something that itched and felt good at the same time. I forgot about what my other friends might think. All I wanted was to sit down somewhere with Lilly and I would tell her everything.

The sky up here on the train platform is yellow from Sibley Boulevard car exhaust, the platform vibrates, and the track whinnies. I'm balancing in high-heeled red sandals and I'm folding the *Tribune* into quarters, the way I've seen the businessmen on the train do it. I'm reading about the Carter-Breshnev SALT talks, trying to understand politics because I'm going to be a journalist. Behind me the giant faces of a blond man and woman fill up a billboard, in love, the god and goddess of perfect blondness, laughing and smoking cigarettes. I don't know how anyone could be stupid enough to think that smoking a cigarette could make you blond and happy, but that seems to be the point. I have to stand with my back to it because it makes me nervous at this close range. There's something scary about too much grinning.

Lilly doesn't always listen to me. If she does, she doesn't always understand. When I'm out with Lilly, she talks more than I do. I'm self-conscious talking to her because sometimes I mumble.

What? What did you say? I can't understand you. Everything in my body starts to itch. If only I could explain things better.

Lilly didn't believe in smoking dope back when we were in high school, so I didn't tell her I loved it. She worried that her little brother was drinking too much, that it was ruining his relationship with their mother. She swore she'd never drink a drop. I thought it was too bad, she was missing out, but I never suggested we drink together. There's always someone to party with. I don't even have to like people to party with them. I saved Lilly for other things.

Lilly's mom hated me. She told Lilly I was a bad influence, a bad kid, like her little brother Billy. Did Lilly know all my secrets without me even telling her? Why would her mother think that about me? We laughed, though, because Lilly loved her brother. We didn't think he was a bad kid. I laughed, and inside I trembled. I was hoping this meant that Lilly loved me too.

Sitting in her kitchen one night, when her mother was out, I told Lilly about a novel by C.P. Snow that I was reading.

"It's so interesting," I said. "The character is old at the end, and he says he doesn't want to read anymore.'' We were eating a loaf of bread that Lilly had baked, the kind you buy as a hunk of dough that keeps in the freezer and all you have to do is heat it up.

"He didn't see the point of learning something new," I continued, "just as he was getting ready to die." This was the kind of novel I loved best, the kind that proves how hopeless it all is, how everything we do is for nothing. The brilliance of this thought reverberated through my mind, another wild guitar riff. Sometimes when I hear this music, I feel like I can see through people, into the truth of everything. It's hard to explain, but it's almost as if my brain is laughing.

"If that's all the book says it doesn't sound like it's worth reading," Lilly said. She didn't say I was worth nothing, but that's how it felt. Lilly's slights gathered on my skin like a rash. Still, there were those times when she aimed that smile of hers at me, so full of promises. As far as Lilly is concerned, I've always had hope.

Anna Karenina jumped in front of a train. It makes me laugh to think of that as I stand here with my ankles trembling, pretending to read this boring newspaper. Maybe Anna Karenina is God. I could stand to believe if that were the truth, her dive into the tracks a resurrection. That's how she became one with the Big Nothing. Too bad I didn't think of this before when I wrote my paper about Anna Karenina for my favorite class last fall semester, the European Novel. "Anna Karenina and Nastasya Filippovna: The Broken Back of Womanhood in the Novels of Tolstoy and Dostoevsky." The T.A. who graded it said I used too many metaphors.

Still, I don't think I got the jumping idea from Anna Karenina. Like I said, it already lived in me. It's an idea natural to my body. It's the *wah-wah-wah* under my skin that's pushing me toward the edge. But remembering Anna Karenina, I can't help but wonder if I'm just trying to be dramatic, and for no good reason. Anna Karenina lost everything and had a whole society against her. Nothing bad ever happened to me. It's not like Lilly. She's the one who has good reason. She's the one who's fabulous and has suffered extreme tragedy and falls in love with the wrong people, like Anna Karenina. *Wah-wah-wah*. Jumping sounds so beautiful.

Lilly's the only one who could have talked me into going to Young Life, the teenage Christian group. Did Lilly know that I didn't believe in God? I never came right out and told her. She may have been trying to convert me. Probably. Anyway, it couldn't have worked. The thought of praying makes my stomach twist up. Even though I respect whatever Lilly wants to believe in, it's stupid to pray to a big old nothing, a bunch of empty particles that hold the earth together like shrink-wrap.

I didn't follow her all the way to the front row. There are some things I just won't do, even for Lilly. I stayed in back and looked at my shoes, making sure no one spotted me. It would just be too much if one of those jolly Christian kids from school came up all happy to see me because they thought I'd reformed or something. I scooted outside as soon as the group leader was done talking. I crouched on the sidewalk outside the storefront where the meeting was held, waiting for Lilly to stop bubbling up to every guy there and come outside to find me.

"I'm never coming here again," I said when she finally caught up with me. Lilly shrugged. Sometimes she treats me like a little kid who just doesn't understand the truth of things.

When we got into her ma's car, she didn't start it up right away, except for the radio. Lilly's face was glowing gold in the passing headlights. A song by Heart came on the radio, *Craaaazy on you*, heavy guitar and girls voices, *crazy crazy on you, crazy on you*. The music was mellowing me out. I stopped being so mad that I'd let Lilly bring me here. I was loving her and watching her golden face when she started talking in this strange way, like she was stoned.

"Last week there was a lecturer I loved," she said. "He told us to think, when we're on a date and kissing, and you know, it starts to go too far? Just think of Jesus, he said, what he gave up on the cross."

She talked quietly, like she was revealing a secret about herself. "If he could give that up for me, I can wait until I'm married."

Why did she believe these things? I didn't tell her that I thought that was a dumb reason. The only reason I can see to stop is that getting pregnant would ruin our chances at having careers. I don't believe in marriage, but I didn't tell that to Lilly either. But there was something else I didn't understand. She really liked making out with boys, much more than I did. She really did have trouble stopping.

That had just happened to me once, the feeling that I couldn't stop, that my body was throwing itself over a cliff and it would kill me if anything got in the way of that falling. That was with the only boy I ever loved, a half-Mexican and half-Polish guy who lived just over the freeway in Calumet City. He had long, straight black hair and pale skin, and he was the best artist I ever knew personally. He drew in charcoal, amazing portraits of his own hands. The night I was sure I couldn't stop, he was rubbing me on the outside of my jeans, and it would have kept going into something, I don't know what, if my little brother hadn't walked in on us. We slipped away from each other, pretended we were just watching TV. It ended so quick, I still wonder if it was real or just something I read about. It never happened again, and then he broke up with me to go out with a short girl who left big purple hickeys all over his long pale neck.

So I knew what Lilly was talking about. It just hasn't been a big problem in my life. Sometimes I wonder if my sex isn't turned up high enough. I have more trouble getting myself to stop playing the same Procol Harum track over and over again, even when I get afraid I'm ruining the record. *Conquistador, your stallion stands, in need of company.* When she talked about this kind of stuff I felt so odd, this private riff in my head rocking louder the more she went on about it. I sat there listening, but my body felt separated from the air around me. *There's no place for me,* that's what it feels like at these times. *I have no place to be, and no one else can hear this damn music.*

My ankles tremble as an Amtrak train approaches fast on the outside track. The urge to jump is a sound—guitars, electric, synthesized tunes, too many notes, too fast. Not my type of music, although I can appreciate its beauty. I prefer less guitar, more words. I like to be able to understand. This music doesn't have any words, except the words the guitar makes, which aren't really words, which is the main problem with it. But the sound is familiar. I hear it all the time, not just on the radio. It's an almost holy sound, but I hate holy. Still, the sound is stuck in me. *Shut up, shut up,* I say to myself, but it's still there, underwater in the shower, in my sleep. I read the paper slowly, mouth each word. The world is a puzzle I can piece together if I can just clear my head.

Lilly left me behind when she went away to college, to Syracuse University, all the way in upstate New York. But not just me. One of those swimmer boys begged her to stay home and marry him. I didn't beg. I understood. She was going to have a career.

She worked at a small radio station the summer before she left, just over the state line in Indiana, a few miles east of the suburbs where we lived. I spent that summer as a lifeguard, scooping little kids out of the diving well at the Harvey Park pool. I dated some of the other lifeguards there, all boys who had gone out with Lilly. I got their attention by talking with them about her. *She said you were a great kisser.* It was true. Lilly said that about most of the boys she went out with.

Except one. He was a blond, but not a swimmer, a party guy, closer to my type. He had shoulder-length hair, wrote poetry, and had a motorcycle. His mission in life was to piss off his father, a Lutheran minister.

"He's rough," Lilly said, before she went out with him. "I want to find out what he's about."

Whatever she found out she wouldn't tell me. Lilly has always had secrets. She never went out with him again. Later that summer, after I went out with him, I said to Lilly, "He's a great kisser."

"No he's not," she said. I was surprised at how mad she sounded. "His lips are too thin and they're cold."

Of course she was right. Why had I said he was great? I didn't mean to lie to Lilly. I liked this guy because he seemed deep, but it was true that he wasn't very friendly. Is this why Lilly didn't like him? Lilly could usually draw out the friendliness in people, but I couldn't. It didn't surprise me when people weren't friendly. But Lilly might never forgive a person for being cold. I had to be on my guard, all the time, to make sure she wouldn't turn on me.

The swimmer guys who worked at the pool asked me out once I let them know I was Lilly's friend. They were the kind of dates where we got drunk and kissed a long time. Then the next day at the pool they wouldn't look at me, not even if I pulled three little kids in a row out of deep water, which happened more than once. I was a great lifeguard. It hurt when they stopped talking to me, but I understood. I wasn't Lilly.

So I stand here looking over the tracks, a too-much-coffee feeling inside my skin. *Why not jump?* I'm not like Lilly; there's no God to stop me. If I try to imagine God, I think of my grandpa's face, all pale and drained of blood, scaring me with his stinking whiskey breath too close to my face. No, the closest thing I have to God is the opposite of God, the flat face of the train, rushing toward me, promising to cut me off from all this noise in my head. I'm standing here, swaying. I can feel the trains come before I can see them. A tickle in my ankles, under all the shaking. I wonder if there's anything out there to reach up, to hold me back.

Lilly's letters from college bugged me. She typed them in all capitals. It made me feel like she was screaming at me over six states. And she acted like her job was to teach me how to live.

MY JOURNALISM PROFESSOR TOLD US NEVER USE THE WORD *VERY* IN A NEWS STORY. IT'S REDUNDANT.

I wasn't so sure she was right about that, but I was careful to avoid it in any letter I wrote her. I felt like crying every time I thought about Lilly being away, but at the same time I was free to spend more time with my party girlfriends. With Lilly gone, I didn't have to worry so much about holding together the person I tried to be when I was around her. Instead, I concentrated on my party education. That's when I first noticed that wine by itself sometimes makes me throw up, and if I smoke pot with more than just one other person around I get paranoid. But if

I do equal amounts of both, it's perfect. My body dissolves into little specks of sand and light, and I'm just one big smile, a part of everything. I wanted to describe this to Lilly, but I never did.

The track is alive, wiggling like the freeway wiggles when I drive home drunk from the North Side bars early on Saturday and Sunday mornings. It's weird, but in these hot moments when I can't decide whether or not to jump, I can see the future. I can see it right now, but in five minutes I'll forget. That's the craziest thing about it. Not that I can see the future but that in five minutes it won't matter because I'll forget what I see. Now, staring down into the tracks I can see me, in six months, lying in a snowdrift, just before dawn, too drunk to stand, staring up at the blank sky, laughing because some people, people like Lilly, think there's a God up there. I see that and I know that's exactly what's going to happen, and it doesn't seem to be anything worth sticking around for. But then I imagine myself as a journalist, slender and without a home, like Lauren Bacall in an old black-and-white movie on late-night TV. I'll wear narrow-cut skirts, smoke tons of cigarettes, blow smoke rings in men's faces to make them fall in love with me. I know that will never happen, but that's the only thing I see.

Lilly changed. Just one year of college did it.

When she came back, right before I graduated, she drank and smoked dope. She was wearing jeans, too, although I still never saw her in a decent rock T-shirt. She still believed in Jesus, but in a different way. She didn't talk about it unless I asked her. I loved the changes in Lilly. There was so much I could tell her now. She was impressed that I had been getting high for years, that I knew where to buy pot and which kind of wine would get you drunk the quickest.

We went to a party together the night after my graduation. The keg and a big metal barrel of popcorn was set up in the garage at the house of another guy who was in love with her. Lilly didn't like him much, but she really wanted to go to this party.

I went to the keg right away, got beers for both of us. Then Lilly spotted two blond guys hanging out by the stereo. I watched her approach, smile at them—that smile that changed her from a plain girl to something else, not a beauty queen, but something golden and slow, a fancy liqueur. The guys had to lean down to hear her. She's short, five-foot-two. The stereo was blasting, a Kansas album, that sad, begging sound I have to be careful not to let in when I'm too stoned to handle it. *Carry on my wayward son. There'll be peace when you are done. Lay your weary head to rest. Don't you cry no more.*

My loving of Lilly tugged at me, in my chest, all rolled up with that crazy Frampton tune I was hearing inside me more and more. Anything could set it off. This time it was the guitar riff from the Kansas song. It tapped me, and my whole body responded. *Wah-wah-wah-wah.* But the weird thing is, the sound in me had somehow become merged with my loving of Lilly. I couldn't tell the difference between them anymore. *Lilly-la-lilly-lo-lilly-la-lilly-lo.* This was the soundtrack of me. I sat in a lawn chair under a clothesline and drank three more beers, fast.

In a few minutes Lilly was back with a report. The guys were older, but not college guys. They had stayed in the neighborhood after graduation, had jobs, paid rent to their parents. I filled my beer cup on the way back to the garage.

It was clear that Lilly wanted the tall, better-looking blond. Unfair, since I'm five-foot-nine and the guy left over was shrimpy. But I wanted Lilly to know I could handle this.

By the time it was dark Lilly had disappeared behind the

garage with the tall guy. I was alone with Shrimpy. He was a skinny guy with wire-rimmed glasses, and his small nose and chin were both a little pointed. He was wearing white shorts, and I didn't like the way his knees looked—sharp-edged, almost pointed. He reminded me of a can opener. We'd been talking for a while, but I couldn't remember a thing he'd said about himself. Before I could prepare, he was leaning up toward me for a kiss. I had just a split second to decide whether to duck away from his skinny lips or to stay still and kiss him back. I thought of Lilly, behind the garage with the tall guy, and I stayed still. His lips were thin as blades.

Lilly came out from behind the garage giggling. I couldn't tell if she was drunk, but I was. When she pulled me into the garage to whisper to me, I stumbled against the popcorn barrel. Popcorn spilled out all over the garage floor, and Lilly laughed. She picked up a handful and threw it over our heads like confetti.

"Let's celebrate," she said, and grabbed another handful. Celebrate what? The new, wilder Lilly? She wasn't really different, just more of everything she was before. She laughed more. She was more lit-up when she smiled. I grabbed some popcorn and threw it toward the clothesline, accidentally hitting Shrimpy in the face. Then I started giggling, and the guy who lived there started yelling at Lilly, looking all heartbroken. "Come on, Lilly. Cut it out. My ma'll have a coronary if you make a mess."

Lilly picked up an armful of popcorn and threw it over her head. We tripped down the driveway to her car, popcorn dropping from our hair.

She took a breath as she started the car. "Why do guys love me so much?" she said, and giggled some more. Then she was quiet, staring out through the windshield at a stoplight down the street that was stuck on red and flashing. I was starting to feel sick to my stomach; the windshield was spinning. I looked at Lilly again, and the spinning slowed down a little. Lilly seemed held by the flashing light. I was held by Lilly. Her face was spinning too, but slowly, like water slipping down the drain.

Lilly started to talk, in that whisper she used when she told me something private and important. I slumped down in the seat to listen better. I loved it when Lilly whispered.

"My father was wonderful," she said. "He loved me so much. I wish I remembered more about him." The car engine idled as she talked. The radio was playing a Heart song, the one that usually I blast if I'm in the car alone. I heard songs by Heart in the car so many times with Lilly that summer I sort of thought of them as our band, even though we never talked about it. *A pretty man came to me. Never seen eyes so blue.* "I was so little when he died," Lilly said. I was listening to her and to the radio both at once. *Try to understand, try to understand.* "That's why I love guys so much." *Try try try to understand. He's a magic man.* "I don't have a father." Then Lilly leaned forward on the steering wheel and accidently nudged the windshield wipers, which started her giggling again.

"There's so much in store for us," she said, as she slipped the clutch into neutral and we rolled down the driveway to the street.

Below the tracks, on Sibley Boulevard, is the roller rink. It's not open at this time of the morning, of course, but isn't it funny to think about some little girls in Brownie uniforms rolling round and round with wheels on their feet while my body falls limp, boneless, onto the tracks? All I imagine is the falling part—that and the train's face scooping me up, sweeping me away like I'm nothing but a pile of dust. Which is the truth. *Ashes to ashes, dust to dust.* The priests in church didn't make that up. We're mostly made up of water, and water evaporates. Not on a humid day like today maybe, but eventually. The human body, if left to evaporate, will turn into nothing but a pile of dust, which proves it to me. God is nothing. We're all just a lot of dust. Maybe I'll just stand here, still as can be. If I blow away before the train pulls in, I won't even have to decide.

Lilly was driving when I told her about the boy who tried to force me. Larry Prystalski. I'd let boys finger fuck me, but I'd never let one screw me all the way. I wasn't exactly against it happening, but not with Larry Prystalski.

I knew Larry from my old job at Geno's Supper Club. I told Lilly how I'd partied with him before, how I just went with him to smoke a joint and talk about the U. of Illinois, where we were both going to college in a couple months.

Lilly didn't say a word while I told her the story, not even to tell me to stop mumbling.

"All of a sudden he was on top of me," I said. "First we smoked and talked about Geno's, and then he started kissing me and I thought, OK, why not, and then all of a sudden he had me pinned against the seat cushion, and I swear his voice changed. He started saying, *Baby baby baby. Don't worry. We'll do this all the time at college.* My arms couldn't move at all. He was really strong."

Lilly still didn't talk. She just kept driving. We were on the freeway, going to the near North Side, to a new bar I'd read about in the *Tribune Sunday Supplement.* "Magic Man" was on the radio again. *Come on home girl, he said with a smile. I cast my spell of love on you, a woman to a child.* That one girl's voice can practically howl. *Magic Ma-a-aaaa-aaaan.*

"Anyway," I said, "he was strong and I couldn't push him off me, and he was starting to unzip my jeans. Then I got this burst of adrenaline and I shoved him away and I rolled right out onto the parking lot pavement. Then I ran. It was weird.''

Lilly's lips were pressed together tight. I couldn't tell what she was thinking. When she did start to talk, she sounded pissed. ''Are you sure you weren't just so stoned that you imagined all this?''

My skin started itching bad when she said that, and the *wah-wah-wah* in my ear got so loud I could barely see her. We were driving through the part of the South Side where the factories are, all open and dried out and dead, the air stinking of sulfur dioxide. It would be at least ten minutes before we could see the lakeshore. Fifteen before we got to the North Side where the bars are.

I found myself trapped in a thought, a memory of me as a little kid, four or five, my dad driving me, on this exact road, home from my grandma's house. There was a box of toys that Grandma kept in her closet for me and my brothers to play with when we stayed with her. I was playing with one—a piece of an old bamboo wind chime, a stick hung with four hollow tubes—when my dad came to pick us up. It made a strange clacking music when I shook it. The noise was empty and long, and the sound of it made me forget everything else. I couldn't hear anything in my whole body when I heard that sound. I couldn't hear the TV my grandma was watching. I couldn't hear my grandpa, all slurry-voiced like there was nothing inside him to hold his words together.

I cried when Dad told me to put it away, so Grandma let me keep it. I clutched it close to my chest all the way to the car. But then when we drove through the part of town where it's all smelly from factories, I decided I hated this toy. I looked at it in my lap, all wood and string, nothing pretty about it. It was stupid. I had to get it away from me. We were stuck in slow traffic when I opened the car door and dropped it. I heard it clack against the asphalt. I knew I was bad to do it. I was a litterbug.

I wasted a toy. But it itched in my hand. I had to get it off me. I got a spanking when I got home, and I didn't even cry. I knew I was bad. I knew I would have nothing, no long, hollow song to hide inside next time Grandpa tried to touch me with his no-color fingers.

Driving by the factories with Lilly, my body was a bucket filled up with this one stupid memory that had nothing to do with anything. The memory spun around inside of me until I was imagining it was not some old toy but my body clacking against the pavement. I thought about opening my car door, rolling away, *clack clack clack clack*, into the freeway traffic, letting Lilly drive away without me.

I hated her as much as I loved her at that moment, but then I remembered that this was Lilly. *Lilly-la-lilly-lo-lilly-la-lilly-lo.* I must have explained it wrong. I must have mumbled.

"Yeah, I was pretty stoned," I said. "Maybe I'll stop party-ing for a while."

Other people are waiting, too, for this train. In fact, it's crowd-ed. It's rush hour. If I move too far to the right or left, I won't have to worry about jumping because someone is sure to jostle me right off the edge.

On the other hand, if I do jump, one of these people could save me. Some guy in a navy blue business suit who thinks he's God might grab me around the waist. Then we'll both fall back-ward, and I'd tumble into his lap. The wind the train makes as it whizzes by will blow the hair off both our faces. Then he'll take me out for coffee, I don't know where. There's no place to go for coffee right around here. We'd have to go up the street to Pepe's Tacos, or down the other way to McDonald's. He'll probably take me to MacDonald's because a guy like that who thinks he's God would worry that I hadn't eaten breakfast. He'll buy me an Egg

McMuffin, and he'll have only coffee because his wife will have made him a big breakfast.

I'll explain that I didn't jump at all, only fainted. I'll tell him I have these mysterious fainting spells where I just crumple up for no reason at all. It's just that it never happened on a train platform before. He'll tell me I'm mysterious and then we'll go a few blocks over to the Stardust Motel. He'll be surprised that I'm not a virgin, but grateful that I have experience. His skin will be so pale-white under his navy suit that at first I'll be afraid to touch it, but then he'll moan with such a deep, low sound that I won't have the heart to stop. He'll pull out of me before he comes, and then he'll sob into my stomach, babbling about his wife and two little kids, and that all he really wanted was to save me. He'll offer me money to see a doctor. To buy myself some more breakfast. Then he'll leave me there, and I'll watch some soaps on the TV and think about how someday I'll write a book about all the guys I've ever slept with.

Lilly met a blond boy she thought she loved. It was at the start of her second year at Syracuse and my first at Illinois. The boy took her to see *Swept Away by an Unusual Destiny in the Blue Sea of August,* an Italian film where a skinny blond woman is trapped on an island with a gristly, dark Italian man that she hates, until he surprises her with sex and then they are in love.

> WE SAW *SWEPT AWAY* AGAIN LAST NIGHT. AND THEN WE WERE SWEPT AWAY, IN THE GRAY WIND OF SEPTEMBER, IN A GRAVEYARD! I LOVE HIM SO MUCH THAT TOMORROW I'M GOING TO THE HEALTH CENTER TO BE FITTED FOR A DIAPHRAGM.

Then everything changed again. Lilly's mother died unexpectedly.

For a long time no one was exactly sure what had happened to Lilly's mom. A neighbor found her dead on the living room rug, her head bloody, an old pipe laying on the floor next to her. They found Lilly's little brother Billy's fingerprints on the pipe. Billy, who was only sixteen at the time, had disappeared. I was away at school when I heard the news. A friend from home who knew I was close to Lilly called to tell me. She'd read it in the newspaper.

I tripped into a white haze. It was October on campus, and the trees were shedding their leaves. I sat in a cushioned pile, their dead smell seeping through my jeans. I hunched over, feeling her in me, gripping my cramped stomach, dizzy with the milky haze and the screaming guitar in the inner corridors of my ears. *Lilly-lo-lilly-lo-lilly-lo.*

I didn't expect her to talk to me at the funeral, but I was there, standing in the rear, staring at the plain, smooth back of Lilly's head. It was a sunny day, but the cemetery seemed shrouded in fog. Lilly seemed shrouded too, like that beautiful, crazy girl who walked the moors in *Wuthering Heights.* I stared at her, wanting so bad to touch her that the tune in my head crashed through me like a concert where the guys start smashing up their guitars. *Lilly-lo.*

I wrote her a note and folded it up in a tight triangle, the way kids in study hall used to fold up math assignments so they could play table hockey.

> call me. i'm in town until monday. call for anything
> at all. i love you.

My whole body shook when I wrote that last part. *I love you.* I'd never said that to her. I'd never said it to anyone. But it seemed exactly right.

The tracks are telling my future again. Staring into the haze
between me and the train's face I see the grassy quad at my college. I am staring at countless girls, my age and older, filing into
an auditorium, the same one where I sat freshman year in World
Mythology 101. The girls are touching and kissing and lighting
matches like people do when a concert is really great, and I'm
getting squirmy in my crotch like I do when I read the lezzie sec-
tions of dirty books. I see hundreds of them, lezzies, listening to
music, but I can't hear it. *What kind of music do lezzies listen
to?* Skin and nipples are visible through thin cotton muscle shirts,
and my lips are aching. If there is a God, maybe this is it. I am
hypnotized by all those nipples, and by the way the train's face
fills up everything as it gets closer, almost a vacuum, sucking me,
sucking me toward the tracks.

"I read the note," Lilly said on the phone. "Thank you for
coming." Her voice was smaller than I'd ever heard it before.
"Of course I came, Lilly."
"It's all so unreal."
"It's very unreal," I said.
"Have you read the papers?"
"I saw a little bit."
"They act like my brother did it. That's crazy. I know he
didn't do it."
I didn't understand why she was so sure. She told me about
the fights between Billy and her mother. "Well, then why is he
gone?" I asked.
"Someone must have broken in. He must be scared. I don't
know. I just know he didn't do it."
I felt guilty for assuming that he had. But Lilly would know,

wouldn't she? The way she said it, she was so certain. What about the fingerprints? I didn't say it. There must have been something I didn't see. "What will you do now?"

"Sell everything. Get out of here. Try to get a message to Billy. He's the only family I have left. Isn't that weird?"

All I heard was that she was leaving. "You're not coming back?"

"I've had enough of the Land of Lincoln," she said. I didn't hear the rest. I couldn't feel the tips of my fingers.

I've never waited so long for a train. What a weird morning. Now I'm remembering a real night, last semester, when I smoked some great pot at a party and then went bar-hopping. It was bizarre at the Red Lion, a bar I hardly ever go to cause it's so heavy metal. But this night we wanted to hit every bar in Campustown. This was the last one on the strip, and I was so drunk I had to sit down right on the corner of the dance floor.

The guys in the band were ugly, stringy-haired, heavy metal freaks. The music sounded like trucks crashing. I saw this guy at the bar—I think it was a guy—his face was pale as an empty movie screen and he was wearing a cape. He was a vampire, I'm pretty sure. Either that or God, the way he'd really look, like someone who loves to suck the life out of everything. I had to stay sitting because the room was wheeling around like a carousel, and I leaned against this metal rail that lined a row of tables where people were drinking. When I looked up I saw this ROTC guy staring at me, and I smiled up at him a little. Then he talked. "Would you like to join us?" I could tell by his voice, it was a girl. A woman with a ROTC haircut. A LESBIAN tried to pick me up at the Red Lion. I'll never forget that. It was the weirdest thing. I got away from her fast and told my girlfriends, screamed it into their ears on the dance floor, but no one believed me. It might not have happened. And I never did find out exactly what that stuff was I smoked.

Lilly's letters changed. She told me how many Coricidin tablets it took to calm jittery nerves. (Three.) And how many would bring on sleep. (Six.) And she listed all the men she'd been with. Love didn't matter anymore, it seemed.

> HE'S 21, A SECOND-YEAR LAW STUDENT WITH
> VERY CURLY HAIR AND BLUE EYES. HE'S TALL,
> BLOND, BLUE EYES, AND BUILT.

Every letter mentioned at least one new guy. And she was still sleeping with the first one, the one she loved.

> LILLY IS HAVING HER CAKE AND EATING IT TOO,
> IF YOU KNOW WHAT I MEAN.

Technically, I hadn't gone all the way with a guy yet. Reading Lilly's letters, I was embarrassed for myself. All the girls I lived with in the dorm thought I was experienced, but I wasn't. The couple of times I'd gritted my teeth and thought, OK, tonight I'm going to go through with this, then the guy I was with couldn't get it up. It happened like this a few times. Lilly never seemed to have this problem.

Months passed before the police found Billy in Key West. Lilly called to tell me about it.

"They're keeping him in Florida, in this home for boys," she said. "It's not so bad, considering."

She never said she thought he did it. She just seemed to accept that Billy lived in this home now. She was relieved to know he was safe. "I'll never stop believing in him."

I wrote her to ask: *How do you stand this?* I couldn't see how she was surviving. Whenever I thought of her the white haze returned and I found myself clutching my stomach. How could she stand to be back in school? How could she stand to breathe?

She wrote me back, and it was all about God.

> I CALL UPON MY BELIEF AND PUT IT TO WORK IN MY LIFE. THE ONLY THING I IMMEDIATELY FEEL IS A PROFOUND INDEPENDENCE, COUPLED WITH A RELIANCE ON THE WILL OF GOD. WITHOUT THIS FAITH THE INDEPENDENCE MIGHT BE OVERWHELMING. I BELIEVE GOD IS READY TO ASSUME FULL RESPONSIBILITY FOR MY LIFE, IF I GIVE IT OVER TO HIM.

I didn't understand. What was she going to do when she realized the truth, that there was no God? That she was giving herself over to a big NOTHING. Would she just disappear?

The train fills up everything. I will never be a journalist. I will dream of Lilly, the way I already dream of her, coming back to Chicago, passing me on the street, avoiding me with her eyes. I will dream of Lilly for years while I sleep, and when I'm awake I will curse her from behind my teeth. The train's face is holy. It sucks in all available light. *Lilly-la-lilly-lo.*

So many men out there, Lilly said to me. I went to see her just this last Fourth of July. I took the train from Chicago to Syracuse, wore my two-inch wood platform sandals, my most faded Levi's, and my hair was newly permed—a style the hairdresser called *sauvage.* I was going to see Lilly for the first time since the funeral. I was so excited I couldn't taste the inside of my mouth.

Lilly's new word was pisser. *Last night we were so drunk.*

What a pisser. *That pot was excellent, a real pisser.* I don't know where it came from, but Lilly said it, so I started saying it, too. I was in Syracuse for four days and for four days I was drunk. What a pisser.

We were sitting at a patio bar, at noon, drinking wine, me wishing I had a curling iron in the car with us because my hair felt flat and I didn't feel pretty enough to be with Lilly. That's when she said it, leaning over the table toward me, her face lit up the way it had been that night in the car when she told me about Jesus on his cross.

"Just think, so many men out there."

After lunch we drove outside of town to watch blond boys dive off rocks into a deep river. My voice was careening a hundred miles an hour inside my own head, but I couldn't manage to say more than a sentence or two at a time. On the trail back from the rocks a man cornered me against a tree, pointing to my breasts, yelling into my face. "Why don't you wear a bra?" I laughed at him, but my nipples felt cold for the rest of the day.

This damned music trapped in me, that's when it got more complicated. Not just guitars, but synthesizers too. Lilly and her friends listened to stuff with lots of horns and multiple voices, like Steely Dan, or that Jerry Rafferty song always playing this summer, with the long weeping saxophone at the start. That's what I heard with my ears, but inside I was electric. It was then I started to know what it was telling me. GO AHEAD. JUMP.

On Saturday we went to Lilly's favorite bar. Lilly ordered me her favorite, a godmother—equal parts vodka and amaretto. Double shots were expensive, but I didn't care if I spent all my money with Lilly. I drank godmothers all night; I don't know how many.

"I'm so glad you're here," Lilly said to me. "It's important to me to have people who knew me before."

I felt tied to her then. We hadn't talked much since I'd been there. Mostly I listened to her tell me about this guy, about that guy. Now it seemed we were moving beyond that, back into the deepness. I wanted to hug her, but instead I just smiled and said, "I think you're doing really good."

Then she was using her whisper voice. "Did you ever think that God has only so much pain for each of us? If that's true, I don't think I'm long for this world."

Me too, me too. But that was ridiculous. Why did I think that? I have no pain. Lilly's the one who knows about pain. Not me. Then some guy started talking to her, and she was laughing, telling him we were CIA agents, in town under-cover. Did he want to see our pistols?

At last call Lilly whispered, "We're going to a party."

She must have driven. I was too drunk to find my way anywhere. The party was in a house where one of the bartenders lived with his parents. I could tell by the decorating scheme in the kitchen—blue-checked pigs and cows in bonnets. There was a keg sitting in a big metal tub in front of the kitchen sink, beer sloshing all over the linoleum. The parents must have been out of town. I was wearing my wooden platforms and was having trouble balancing, so I got a beer and leaned against the wall in the foyer where a bunch of people who looked strangely familiar were standing. Were they from the bar? All the lights were on, and it seemed strange to see people's faces. I didn't know where Lilly was.

Jimmy Buffet was playing somewhere in the house. *Wasted away again in Margaritaville. Looking for my lost shaker of salt.* A guy talking to me looked like Jimmy Buffet, tall and a little chunky with messy blond hair. He must be really tall, I thought, if he's taller than me in my platforms. He said he was a lacrosse player. I asked him what that was but I didn't hear what he said. He was showing me an ID with his picture on it, I don't know why.

"Are you trying to prove you're a natural blond?" I asked him, and then I couldn't stop laughing.

Pretty soon he was whispering to me. I couldn't see Lilly anywhere. He wanted me to go with him to a back room.

"I can't," I said. "I'm a virgin." Then I started laughing again because I couldn't believe I'd said that to him.

"Don't worry," he said, "I won't go all the way."

He was the type of guy Lilly would appreciate. I wondered if this was what Lilly saw when she thought about God. Anyway, he was blond. I hoped she'd gotten a look at him.

We went to a dark room with two twin beds. I don't remember laying down, taking off my clothes, or anything else, except his penis vanishing into me. It felt like nothing.

Oh, I thought, and wondered why it seemed I could see his naked ass, my naked breasts and thighs. I wondered why it seemed like I could see his penis going into me, when all the time he was on top, covering me with his wide, loose stomach.

What a pisser. That's what I was thinking, about the word pisser, how it could mean PENIS. Is that what Lilly meant?

When he was done he groaned a little. Then he smiled at me. Even though he'd lied, he seemed like a pretty nice guy.

"You have natural ability," he said. "Did you come?"

Oh. I was supposed to have an orgasm. I thought about lying, but I always swore I'd never be the type to fake it.

I reached for my clothes. The little dark room was giving me the creeps. All I could think was how gross it would be the next day when someone found the sheets we'd been on.

"You didn't come?" his voice was a little bit whiny. "You should have told me. I could have made you come."

"That's OK," I said, and I zipped up my pants, slipped on my platforms. I was having trouble getting air into my lungs.

When I got up to leave he was still lying naked on the bed, his long soft penis curled up over one thigh. "Hey, wait a second," he called out.

I paused with my hand on the doorknob. "Will I have to worry about the pitterpatter of little feet?" he asked. He had a cute look on his face. I wondered if he practiced that look in the mirror.

The idea of babies wouldn't even materialize in my mind. "Don't worry about it," I said, and I slipped out the door.

There were a couple of big blond guys passed out in the hall when I got there. I found Lilly lying on the living room couch, smoking a cigarette.

"Come on," she said. "I have to get some sleep."

In the car we were quiet. I had expected something different, giggling or congratulations. "Did you see the guy I was with?" I asked.

"I saw a lot of guys."

"I'm not a virgin anymore," I told her. It was an offering. If there had been a candle at her feet I would have lit it. That's how it felt, like I was giving this to her. She said nothing.

When she finally talked she said, "Listen." We pulled up in front of the wood duplex where she lived with two roommates and her mother's old color TV and brocade furniture. She kept the car running, and a Bonnie Koloc song was playing. *There are few blue-eyed men I would choose to believe, in this wide world round. But if I were on the ocean, the waves all around me, I'd roll, baby, right back in your arms.*

I thought Lilly was telling me to listen to the song, that we were sharing something here, so I was surprised when she kept talking.

"I don't want to be gross," she said, "but those sheets on the spare bed are new. Please don't get blood on them. OK?"

I stared at her in the dark. My body was itching in places I'd never felt before, between my legs, up my crotch. I felt an awful stickiness dripping from me. I thought about what that guy said, about pitterpatter, and I wondered what I would do if I were pregnant. But I knew I wasn't pregnant. The flesh between my waist and thighs felt dead as bologna. What was Lilly so mad about? All I could think of were the cliffs we'd seen earlier that weekend, the blond boys diving. I imagined the car we were sitting in sailing off the side of one of those cliffs, smashing head first onto the rocks.

I didn't bleed on the sheets. I didn't bleed at all, which made me wonder if I'd imagined the whole thing. Lilly took me to a bar for lunch and a disco after dinner. We didn't talk about it. My train left at 2:00 A.M., and I was drunk when I got on it. I watched Lilly out the window as the train pulled out, her shape spotting away in the darkness. *Lilly-la-lilly-lo.* The synthesizers and guitars had never been louder, and I wondered whether the train windows opened, if I could fit through them, fall out, dead as bologna on the tracks. Lilly was gone. *Shut up. You're a crybaby when you're drunk,* I told myself, but something in me knew I wouldn't see her again. Her shape in the window was replaced by the reflection of my face.

I'm staring down at the tracks, inching closer. *Go ahead. Jump.* In my head I am shouting back at the tracks. *I am going to be a journalist.* I try to see myself in a slim-cut suit, smoking cigarettes. I don't know why, since I don't even smoke cigarettes, but I try to see me, smoking and typing an important story onto the VDT screen. But that's not what I see. I see myself at thirty, on my knees in the street and not even drunk, purposely not drunk, trying not to drink, who knows why, and mouthing what I think are prayers, not because I believe in prayers, but only because trying to believe seems to be keeping me alive. Like it kept Lilly alive. *I call upon my belief. God is ready to assume full responsibility.*

I am shocked to see myself praying. *That's stupid,* I shout back. *If I want to see God I'll just have another drink.* But the picture continues, and I know it will happen. Someday I will pray. Not to God. Not to a big blond boss, like what Lilly believes, but to something real out there, to hold me.

I can't stand the thought of it but I know it could happen. I could turn into someone who PRAYS to keep from jumping, and believe me, this is the scariest thought I've had all morning.

Stories about Lilly started spreading a few weeks ago. This was after I got her letter.

> I MET A GUY. WE'RE GOING TO D.C. FOR THE
> WEEKEND, TO *DO IT* IN STYLE, YA YA YA. IT'LL
> BE A PISSER.

Then I heard she'd been in Chicago, didn't tell any of her friends she was here. It was the weekend that one of Lilly's oldest friends got beat up by her husband, an ex-cop. Lilly was the woman he ran off with. I didn't understand. Guys could do anything, and Lilly still believed in them.

Her last letter was written on the stationery of some senator in D.C.

> HELP! WHERE ARE YOU?

I recognized her style. It wasn't a cry for help, just another tease, like that smile that started me loving her in the first place. I wrote her back.

> why did you do that? why did you run off with a
> wife-beater? do you care about anyone? how could
> you come to chicago and not even call?

I admit, not very friendly. She didn't write back. It was the first time I asked a question she didn't answer. I shouldn't have said it that way, I know. Lilly would think it was cold. Where am I? Getting ready to jump.

So go ahead. Jump. What keeps me from it? I don't want to stay here. I don't even want to be a journalist. I suppose Lilly MIGHT still write me back. It doesn't matter. Nothing holds me except thinking ahead. Friday night in the Rush Street bars, that will happen. What else?

I'm thinking about jumping, and the longing comes up out of my body, a rapid, screaming soundtrack amplified from the inside of my ears. Then it's weird, but I think about my favorite album. Rick Wakeman. He's the synthesizer guy for Yes. He made this solo album, all synthesizers, about the wives of an old king from England. This king had six wives and he offed them all—a real maniac. But the thing is, this album has no words. The whole album's a story, but there's not one word. I have to THINK about that, why I LOVE this album when it doesn't have a single word. The train pulls up. I climb on.

I sit down on an orange vinyl bench seat, peer out the tiny streaked window at all the backyards and back steps and garbage cans of the South Side neighborhoods. I can't see the blue praying hands from here, but I can see the big yellow smiley face on the Cal City water tower. I'm thinking about after work, how I need to listen to that album, how I wish there were some way I could listen to it now. Riding along I try to reconstruct it in my head, but it's too complicated, too hard to keep all the sounds together. This will take the utmost concentration. The train bumps along the commuter line, the old Illinois Central, and I ride it, all the way to the last stop downtown.

the kiss

The first time Angela kissed me I didn't kiss her back. I'm not the kind of woman who would kiss Angela, I thought. That bar-dyke, I thought. That jock.

She had the widest thumbs I'd ever seen on a woman, wide and squat with only a thin strip of nail. I am not attracted to those thumbs, I thought. Her fingers were not mildly scented with lotion. Her nails were bitten short, her knuckles rough and chapped. I am not attracted to masculine women, I thought.

I loved Irena, who painted. She painted wild, blurry watercolors, a million different versions of her own face. Her paintings were mostly orange, which usually I hate, but this orange was sweet, the taste of Dreamsicles. I loved Irena's paintings and I loved Irena's face, so round and laughing, and I loved the ring she always wore on her plump middle finger, a silver molding of Isis, the winged goddess. And her hair was unruly and so black, like crazy, black rushing water. "Your hair, it's really black," I said, the first time I touched it.

"Yes," she said, a little bit sweet, a little bit patronizing. "I have black hair and I'm a Jew."

At the start she wouldn't let me forget she was nine years older. Later, when I hurt her by falling in love with Angela, her attitude changed. Then she was pure feeling, a long squall. "How

81

can you touch me after you've had your fingers in her?" Her face reddened, crumpled up like used wrapping paper. I couldn't answer her. It wasn't my fingers in Angela that I thought of. I thought of Angela's fingers in me.

When I began to take women as lovers, I thought I loved them because they were like me. "I do not believe in butch and femme roles among lesbians." I said it gravely. "We are equal, and so we can't hurt each other the way men hurt women." That is what I said. I was twenty-three-years old, and able to say all things seriously because I knew so little about myself, about what I desired and about what desired me.

But I did secretly imagine myself some kind of butch. I had, after all, once taken the cylinder head out of my car. It took me six months, partly because I was stoned the whole time, mostly because I hated doing it. Still, I had done it. My fingers had stroked the inner regions of a car engine.

I was twenty-one when I started stripping away anything that straight people, especially men, might consider female. If I spotted any fleeting bit of the surface accoutrements of a femme in me, I pinned it down, interrogated it under a murderous light. Then I used the jackhammer.

Do I want to wear a dress? *Rat-atat-atat-atat.* I wear pants. Baggy pants.

Do I want to wear lipstick? *Rat-atat-atat-atat.* Make-up is demeaning.

Do I want to wear a bikini? *Rat-atat-atat-atat.* I bought a one-piece black tank suit at Goodwill, the kind they used to make us wear in high school P.E.

It was 1982 and the lesbianism I followed was invented in the seventies. From all the movement songs and magazines, one could only assume that all real lesbians were butch. So Angela was butch. I was butch. We were all butch, and yet somehow I suspected that two butches together just wouldn't work. One of us would have to fall. I would not fall, not for anyone, and Angela, with her short, uncombed curls, her stolid, boyish body, her cowboy gait, she wasn't going to fall.

So, we would be friends. We leaned over one of the narrow particle board desks of the theater company office where we both worked and introduced ourselves. I bummed a cigarette, even though Winstons made my throat ache, and she told me about the woman she lived with then, Marie, a cute blonde who wore mini-skirts. "We're young, but we're enduring," Angela said, and I nodded, as if I knew all about love.

I wonder, did every new kiss change me? I had my first at age fifteen with a boy on the beach in Mexico. My parents were schoolteachers with whole summers off work, and my father was hungry to see the world. Summers we drove, all five of us and a German shepherd dog. In Manzanillo I met Humberto, an older boy, nineteen, who lived with his sister in a house at the precipice of the mountain that cradled the bay where we camped. He slipped down a mile of serpentine stone steps to the sand beach to see me every night. "*Te quiero mucho*," he whispered as he pressed his lips into mine and slid one hand under my bathing suit top to massage my breast. I pressed my lips back against his, not too hard, waiting to taste the soft snake of his tongue. My breast felt rubbery and too loose in his palm, and he scratched me with the tiny rocks of sand that were stuck in the damp creases of his fingers. He is kissing me, I thought.

Later I let high school boys fondle my breasts and sometimes my nipples wrinkled to crepe points between their fingers, but my interest in petting was purely scientific. So this is what happens to nipples when they're too cold or stroked. So this is how a boy's breath sounds when his head knocks against my collarbone. Sometimes I'd let them slip a finger into my opening. It usually took them a while to find it. I didn't help. Their fingers scrambled like spiders through my wiry bush until they found the hole and dove in to find—what? I was never sure why they moaned and squirmed. *Finger-fucked,* the girls whispered to each other. *He finger-fucked me in his car at the forest preserve, after we had beers. We smoked a joint in the garage, and then he finger-fucked me.* Technical virgins we called ourselves, terrified of pregnancy but still longing for the highs promised by dirty books and R-rated movies.

Once I drank a whole bottle of Mad Dog wine with my half-Polish, half-Mexican boyfriend Jimmy Martinez. We were in his car, parked in the lot behind the girls school—St. Mary the Immaculate. That was the only time I bothered to crawl into the backseat first. By 1976 backseat make-outs seemed cliché, so we usually fumbled around in front, bumping the clutch and steering wheel. In the wide, rocking bed of the backseat, lit yellow from the Calumet City street lamps, I was more enthused than usual. Mad Dog jolted me all at once, a violent rush, and we'd chugged it down like Coca-Cola. I yanked my jeans down to my knees and he finger-fucked me. I was bored by his skinny finger spiraling around inside me like a lost June bug. I tried to push his head down between my thighs, to my screaming desire to be kissed on the clit. He jerked his head back, a horse rejecting the rein. "No way."

Still he didn't try to put his penis in me. Perhaps he was as bored with the thought of intercourse as I was. I loved him because he was an artist. I wrote smoky poems with titles like "Don't Tie Me Down," and he drew exquisite sketches of his own long-stemmed hands. But when he refused to kiss me below the belt, he put a rift in our delicate artists' union. I went home and threw up the Mad Dog, then felt desperately abandoned.

After Jimmy, I loved no one—except when I was kissing. It could happen with anyone, but when rough fingers dropped to my nipples or crotch, I lost my true love, gone in one sudden electric jolt, and it was replaced with science. Is this how much fire it takes to bend a glass tube? Will this size finger fit in me? I met these boys at parties. We didn't have to know the host or even be invited. All that was needed was parents out of town and a rumor. Party tonight. One of these guys I met by the keg while Pink Floyd throbbed from the phonograph. *I'll see you on the dark side of the moon.* We smoked a joint, then went to his car. He kissed me, open-mouthed, and sucked blood roses out of the tissuey skin of my neck while I swooned love, oh love, oh love. But once he stopped kissing, the music ground out, became the rusty groans of regular breathing. I thought, something is dead in me. Why can't I hold onto a feeling?

That jackhammer, I really did see it once. It was in a photograph, in a porn magazine. The woman in the photo was blond, her hair languid and shimmering, like Mod Squader Peggy Lipton's hair. Just like Peggy Lipton, the woman's hair hung over her shoulders, straight as rain. She wore a yellow bra with beaded fringe, but her crotch was bare. She lay on her back, propped up on her elbows, looking over her shoulder into the camera. Her legs stuck up into the air, split apart, a wide open V, her crotch exposed. Between her legs stood a man with a jackhammer pointed into her vagina. My body went as dead as a burnt-out bulb when I saw the photo. *This is shock,* I said to myself, and I heard a crackle. The man smiled, and the woman puckered her red lipsticked lips. The jackhammer raped her while yellow beads swung from her yellow bra.

A lot changed after I saw this. I told Leonard, my last boyfriend, that I would not let him put his penis in me again. Not in my mouth, not in my vagina, not anywhere. OK, I agreed, I would still touch his penis. But touching was the limit. Every

penis that had ever been in me felt like a jackhammer. Just thinking of it my flesh flicked off, cold.

I was twenty and lived in the middle of Illinois. I'd moved
from the near south suburbs of Chicago to this tiny college town
surrounded by corn two years earlier, when I was a freshman
at the University of Illinois. By the time I was twenty I'd dropped
out of school and was waitressing a split shift at the Round Barn,
a steakhouse at the edge of town where I wore a German milk-
maid's dress and learned to mix martinis. Every night after work
I stretched out alone on my Salvation Army mattress and smoked
the Kool butts Leonard left in my ashtray, or skinny brown Trues
from the cigarette machine at the restaurant. I drank Chablis
or Schwarze Katz Liebfraumilch until I was drunk, while scratchy
Joni Mitchell crooned from the stereo. *You are in my blood like
holy wine, you're so bitter and so sweet. I could drink a case of
you, and I would still be on my feet.*

I didn't call Leonard nights after I worked. He was non-
monogamous, so no telling who he might be with. I lived on the
edge of campus, in the basement of a crumbling old house where
the walls were always a little bit damp and cockroaches thrived
in the cabinets among my chipped dishes. Three students lived
on the floor above me. A dark-haired hippie boy who taught me
how to buy granola in bulk. A sandy-haired Jewish boy who
drank wine with me some nights on the cracked front steps and
once admitted that he might love me. And curly headed Greg,
hairy-chested, burly for only age eighteen, and purportedly gifted,
the son of college professors.

I slept with Greg once, on a night when Leonard was off with
some other lover. He climbed down into my basement, and we
drank white wine and played Joni Mitchell albums. In bed he
pressed his hefty hips flat into my skinny ones and whispered,
''What do you want out of life?''

''I want to write poetry,'' I whispered back.

"Why?"

"To make beauty."

"Ah," he said, and his penis was erect. He pushed my arms over my head and held them there with one elbow as he fucked me. I hope he won't stay all night, I thought, as I listened to Joni Mitchell wail. *I am on a lonely road and I am traveling, traveling, traveling.*

Soon after I saw the jackhammer.

I had already been thinking of lesbians, suspecting I was one of them, not sure I could stand to be one of them. My introduction to lesbian culture was partly Leonard's doing. I was nineteen when I met Leonard. I was working in the kitchen of a campus bar and grill where I stacked dishes into an industrial dishwashing machine that filled the airless room with so much steam the lenses popped out of my glasses. Leonard was an itinerant handyman. He was there to adjust the plumbing. When he smiled at me, I noticed the gray streaks in his beard. The next time I saw him he was in the bar, at night, sitting alone with a pitcher of beer, wearing a gray beret, smoking Kools, writing on a yellow legal pad. He looked like someone radical and important, like a lawyer for the Weather Underground, or if not that, perhaps a novelist. A novelist! The thought of it made me quiver, and some part of me cried out, *Feed me, feed me, please.*

It turned out he was a graduate student. What he was writing was his dissertation. Close enough, I thought. The first time I went out with him we drank several pitchers of beer and he smoked a pack of Kools. "My theory is that those of us who did a lot of LSD in the sixties need a lot of menthol to keep us going today," he told me. He was thirty-two.

"The day I turned thirty I went down into the basement and cried," he told me. I thought that once a person turned thirty all the cells of personality and talent gelled. Once you are thirty you are complete, I thought. At nineteen I had a lot of respect for thirty.

When he parked his 1965 Volkswagon Squareback in front of my dorm, I leaned over and kissed him, thrusting my tongue into his mouth. "Whoa," he said.

"What?" I cringed back away from him, pressed my back into the rusted door handle. I was used to drunk kissing, just tripping into it, and I was a little drunk after all that beer. He was not drunk, not yet. I didn't know then that most nights he preferred to get drunk at home. I was still a wild, outdoor drunk.

"What are you doing, sticking your tongue in my mouth like that?"

"You're thirty-two. I thought that's what you'd be used to."

That made him cough and laugh at the same time. Inside me a crazed longing was pumping. *I'm sorry. Feed me, feed me. I'm sorry.*

"Would you like to spend the night with me?" he asked, still laughing but looking at me tenderly. I saw there was some complex etiquette involved here. I wasn't sure what the right answer was. "Do you want to?" I stammered.

He laughed again. "You're sure full of mixed messages." Bile rose in my throat. I had used the only move I knew how to play. A kiss. Now I was feeling nauseous and wanted to sleep. It seemed to me obscene to discuss sex before you did it. If I stopped to think, it only disgusted me. I was used to sex just happening. I went in alone.

The next time I saw him we went to a new bar, a place called Mabel's, where the main floor was covered with giant overstuffed cushions instead of tables and chairs. We sat on a carpeted stairway leading up to a balcony that hung over the main floor. Leonard balanced the pitcher of beer on the step between his big old scruffed hiking boots. "I wanted you to see this band," he told me, nodding toward the stage. "They're friends of mine."

The band members were all women. I'd never seen an all-woman band. The singer was tall with long frizzy hair. She introduced herself to the crowd—Mary Kowalski. I'd seen her before, in the bar where I worked, dancing on top of a table with another woman. What is that? I thought when I saw it. I supposed they were queers, but I didn't want to assume. On this night, with the band, she wore cowboy boots, and between songs held a baby. Something thrilled me about those cowboy boots, the way her jeans hugged her thighs and flared open slightly around the buffed brown leather. Watching her I sweated a little.

"They're all lesbians," Leonard whispered.

His friends were lesbians? "But she has a baby?"

He laughed again, that coughy, throaty laugh, and I could feel myself blush in the dark. "You should know," he whispered, moving closer, "I'm bisexual."

Bisexual! Bisexual!

I said, "Oh really?" I didn't want to hear that laugh again, and so I tried to sound bored. I sat next to him, quietly, in the smoky dark, feeling as if one thousand pins had pricked me all at once.

It was dark on the staircase. I couldn't see the faces of the people who passed us on their way to the upstairs bar. One of those people—I couldn't tell if it was a man or a woman—leaned over and tweaked Leonard on the shoulder. Leonard grabbed hold of the person's hand and squeezed. They both laughed, low secret laughs that left me outside. Leonard let go of the hand and the person disappeared up into the smoky crowd.

I had been transported to a whole new country. Lesbians with babies. Bisexuals who nudged each other in the dark.

Yes, I thought, and opened my mouth in the smokey dark, *Yes, yes, let me drink this.* I leaned into the red iron rail on the stairway, sucked from my beer, and then cradled it between my knees. I sat there, alone with myself, watching the lesbians sing.

That night I went to bed with Leonard.

"Your breasts are nicer than I expected," he said.

I was afraid to say anything. He had housemates. What if they heard me? Leonard pulled me on top of him. "You feel so good," he said smiling. I ran my hands through his chest hair. Is this what they liked? I'd read in a magazine that men were aroused when massaged at the small of their back, but I couldn't think of anyway to maneuver my hand back there without calling too much attention to myself.

I had been with a lot of men. Their faces were blurred, their names unmemorable. I hadn't loved any of them, but they'd all been in me. I was the most experienced girl I knew, but sex still felt so odd to me. I told my women friends that I loved sex, loved men. I wanted them to think I was a fast girl, and they did. I tried to believe it too, or at least thought if I kept practicing, it would get better. I had expected to be in love by now. There were moments, when I met a man at a party or a bar, when I pursed my lips slightly, or ran one finger, pretending I didn't mean to, along the bottom line of my lower lip, and I felt the man move toward me slightly. A few more drinks and I felt my body loosen within my skin. If he leaned over and touched my leg or my arm, I tingled—not with pleasure, but with some other sort of rush, some *whoosh* that felt like power. He wants to touch me. The *whoosh* caught in my throat and I trembled. I am in love. By this time I was too drunk to focus on the man's face. He walked me to some room with a bed. Sometimes we had to trudge outside through snow to get there, the man all the while whispering, "I'd like to strip you and wrap you in clean white sheets. I'd like to dip you in chocolate and suck." Tap beer and this feeling that seemed to be love *whooshed* through me, a tornado of spinning emotion that sucked me inside its whorl. From that point on I forgot everything. Except, sometimes, a bird's eye view of a stranger pumping his penis in me. In the morning, or maybe even later that night, the *whoosh* became a sick, dizzy spinning. The air crinkled with static and chill. They said a girl was supposed to feel dirty after a one-night stand, but that's not what I felt. It was more of a drone, a monotone buzz. What did it mean? Nothing. What did anything mean? Nothing.

Leonard's penis was hard, and he was smiling up at me. I could barely feel the beer under my skin.

"Please, stay on top," he whispered. What did he mean? What was I supposed to do? He tried to guide his penis into me, but I was uncertain. Would he just slip it in? Was there some technique, some method I should know? I wasn't used to feeling so— what? Awake. I felt too awake for this.

"What's wrong?" he whispered. I was caught. I should have faked it, figured it out. "You look worried," he said.

"I've never done this before, in this position," I admitted. He stared at me, blinking. Then he laughed, and his belly rattled beneath me. How could I get out of this? I had no clothes on. I couldn't just get up and leave. His penis was still erect. He rolled me over and came inside of me. Later, he clutched me between damp sheets, kissed me on the forehead, and whispered, "Thank you. Thank you. I've been impotent for months."

My body cured his impotence, made his dick stand up straight for the first time in months? I knew he thought he was complimenting me, but I was disgusted. But did his penis feel like a jackhammer? I can't say it really felt like anything, just a rubbing I disliked between my thighs, and I would have thought it happened to someone else except the soft flesh at the top of my thighs felt raw.

Yet, he did seem to like me. And he went down on me, gave me orgasms. Up until then I'd given all my orgasms to myself, with my own hand, alone under the sheets in my fold-out bed. Then Leonard started giving them to me with his tongue. I liked

the slow leak of tension out of my body, and being able to relax, just wait for it.

But his penis, it always stung.

Leonard had lesbian books in his room. I read *Rubyfruit
Jungle* in his bed one Sunday morning while he read the paper.
We drank cinnamon tea, smoked cigarettes, and I finished the
book before we got up. By Sunday afternoon I was begging him
to tell me how it felt to him when he went down on me. Later,
alone in my own apartment, I laid on my bed and closed my eyes,
conjuring up each girl I had admired in high school, imagining
what it would be like to spread her legs, run my fingers through
her hair, lean close, run my tongue along the ridge of her vulva.
And then I imagined what it would be like to kiss her there.

I learned from Leonard where to find lesbians. The National
Women's Music Festival was held on the Illinois campus every
summer, and another lover of Leonard's was one of the organizers. I went to the concerts alone, sat in the back row, and
I felt like I had a fever every time I saw women in the dark rows
ahead of me lean into one another and kiss. When I looked at
the festival calendar, I saw that lesbians were women who were
against things. There were workshops called Women Against Nuclear Energy, Women Against Rape, Women Against Capitalist
Patriarchy. I chose the Women Against Pornography slide show
because I knew slides required a room without lights. I didn't
want anyone to see me or talk to me. I just wanted to watch.

I sat in a back corner chair with no one seated to either side
of me. Mary Kowalski, from the lesbian band, was there, seated
two rows ahead. It had been more than a year since I'd seen her.
Her frizzy hair was half stuck in her collar, and through the back
of her folding chair I watched how her jeans stretched taut over
her hips and butt when she leaned forward. I was sure it was
Mary when I spotted her boots—tawny, golden leather, snug over
her toes, and bent to a silver-tipped point. I wanted to get down

on my knees and stroke those boots, squeeze her shin until the leather collapsed under my fingers and I could feel what must surely be a tough, muscled calf. I watched her back as the lights dimmed.

But once the slides began I forgot her. Illuminated on the screen I saw a naked woman, her thighs and red decorated toes pressed together, her head vanished into the open jaw of a meat grinder, ground meat twirling out the other end.

I saw a drawing of a naked, misshapen woman with greasy string hair, narrow hanging breasts, bumpy thighs, and rats crawling out of her vagina.

I saw the blond woman raped by a jackhammer.

I was drawn to this torture, despite my revulsion, huddled around this filmy yellow light, a white moth caught in a dirty lantern. No one would want a jackhammer in her vagina. I didn't want any more penises in me. Finally, here was something I could point to. *Look, this is how it feels to be me.*

Many times Leonard had asked me why I had let so many men fuck me. "I know how men are," he said. "How could you let them use you?" For the same reason I let *you* fuck me, I thought. But why? Because I loved lacy underwear? Because I wanted to wear that yellow bra with swinging, beaded fringe? Wanting this, did it mean I wanted the jackhammer?

No, I would kill everything men like. I would murder whatever made any man want to fuck me. Let's kill all the girly-girly things. Let's kill that rainy-haired blond who whispers, *Spread open, spread open your thighs.*

I thought I had the answer the first time I kissed a woman. It was that singer, Mary Kowalski. My first thought was how soft, such soft, soft lips. "Yes, I thought you'd notice that," she said, and kissed me again.

Later Mary and I kissed in a crowded room of straight people as the Supremes screamed, *STOP, in the name of love.* It was at a party thrown by a collective household of community organizers and graduate students. A co-worker of mine, one of the community organizers who lived there, had a little girl who asked her, "Why are those two ladies kissing?" Her mother told her, "Because they love each other," but the truth was I was not in love. Mary, naked, did not excite me the way she did in her blue jeans and boots, and I was too bashful then to ask her to wear leather to bed. I liked the zing I felt when her pink nipples nudged my wide brown ones, but she did not pull her weight over me, she did not push open my quivering thighs, she did not shiver like a foil mobile and delve into me with her open mouth. Instead, being feminists, politically correct, we were polite, not butch, not femme, just naked androgynes with soft, soft lips and and sweet pillow breasts. We pinched softly and left no marks when we sucked. I came in breathy pink clouds; she hardly came at all. This was very fun, no jackhammer here, but I still found myself standing back, observing—so this is lesbian sex.

I was not positive I was going to be with women until I moved to Minnesota and kissed Irena.

Kissing her the first time I noticed it again. The softness of the lips. I kissed her before she kissed me. I leaned over to where she sat cross-legged on the cheap blue carpet with its long unravelling threads and said, in a whisper, "Once I drove all the way around Lake Superior, in Canada, by myself in a '73 Pinto. I drove into the bushes at night and slept in the back of the car."

As I had hoped, she was impressed. She cried a bit, a few glittering tears down her pale cheeks. She said, "I have never been brave." I said, "I like to do things that scare me," and then I kissed her. She kissed me back, and we spent the next day on my futon with its down comforter and Indian print spread. What I remember is making love to her, pressed on top, my long fingers

in her cunt. Finger-fucked, I thought, and laughed, but didn't
tell her why. I treated her as I wanted to be treated, taking
charge, pulling out her loud, wily orgasms over and over again.
She made love to me gently, as if too rough a thrust would shatter
me, and I can see why she would have thought I needed such
care. I was a brittle, silent girl, twenty-three and pretending to
be worldly. A woman who held herself so tight might crack apart
at any unexpected surge.

"It's powerful, making a woman come," she said to me, but
I denied that the rush I felt was power.

"No, no, it's just that I love you."

Oh, I liked it, but not as much as I would have liked getting
it back. I knew then I was queer, but still, I craved a cowboy. I
thought to have it, I had to be it myself.

Three years later Angela kissed me. We were standing in the
parking lot of the building where Angela lived with Marie who
was, by then, only one of her lovers.

"I can't leave her," Angela moaned, lurching between the
parked cars, purposely stomping through puddles of melted
snow. It was March, still winter in Minnesota, but thaw had come
early. The sky drizzled, and the wet pavement glistened in the
light of street lamps and the headlights of slow-moving cars.

"Which one?" I asked her, shambling behind. We had been
drinking in a neighborhood bar with women from the theater
where we worked, discussing Catholicism and how to quit smoking. Irena, the one I loved, was working in Boston for who knew
how long. Thousands of miles away, in Minnesota, I had no idea
how to wait for her return.

"The thing that's Catholic," I had explained to one of the
actors, "is that I want to call her tonight, but I'm sure I shouldn't.
I'm sure I should wait and suffer a little longer."

"I can't quit smoking," Angela had said, leaning into the face
of the touring manager, who took a drag from one of her long,
greeny Eves before she replied. "We could quit if we chose to
quit."

Gretel, who had just begun to sleep with Angela, rolled her
eyes. "I'm tired." The dim bar lights rippled through her hair.
Gretel was not the best actor of the bunch, but she was really
pretty. Rising from her seat, in the smokey light, she looked like
an aloof movie star. She thinks we like to look at her, I thought,
which of course, we did.

"Good night," she said, in a dusky voice. She wrapped her
Guatemalan shawl around her shoulders and left without saying goodbye to her lover.

This steamed Angela. "Off to see her boyfriend. Damn
straight girls." She lit another cigarette and swallowed the rest
of her beer, then returned shouting to the smoking debate.
"Don't tell me what I can choose or not choose to do. What's
choice anyway?"

Angela and I were the last in the bar, and when we left I was
dying for food. Now, slogging after her through the parking lot,
I said, "Angela, please, let's eat. I never got dinner."

Angela ran ahead, sliding through the narrow corridors between cars. "What am I supposed to do?" she shouted into the
melting night. I wasn't sure if it was Gretel or Marie she was worried about.

"I can't end it with Gretel," she said. "It's too hot. Did I tell
you what she said about this drizzle?" She held her face up into
the fine spray. "She said it's the sky having tiny, sputtering orgasms." Angela stood with her pale moony face lifted, and she
shuddered.

"So it's Marie you want to leave?" Instead of answering me,
she started to run, crash-bombing a car bumper in the next
parked row. How much beer had Angela had? She jumped

straight up and landed both feet on the bumper. The first car was small, a Honda. It just squeaked a bit, and she bounced back down to the pavement. The next one, a rusted Volaré, rocked and creaked. When she popped off the front of an old Buick wagon, the bumper moaned.

Angela moaned too. "I'll miss her little duck face."

Then she stood still, facing me, her curls damp and multiplied in the rain, her eyes bright as headlights. I had been drinking vodka tonics and felt full of too many edges: the edge of my hip bones rubbing against the belt of my jeans, the sharp edge of my shoulder blades breaking out of the torn collar of my sweatshirt. Puddle water seeped through the seams of my tennis shoes, and I felt my damp hair friz in the faint drizzle. Angela looked amazing, neon as a bar marquee, flashing blue and red, blue and red, the kind of cold-hot glow you can feel all the way into bone. Still, I wasn't thinking of kissing her. I was thinking how I wished I could move my body like that, loose and courageous as a boy on a skateboard. I wondered how it felt to be so square and mannish but still a woman, and never, ever fine-edged and brittle and afraid.

I stood silent, my head throbbing a little, and I watched the red-blue light fill and drain from her round, white face.

When Angela leaned her moony, flashing face into mine, I pushed her away. It wasn't loyalty to Irena that stopped me. What I feared was the loss of control, the return of that beaded yellow bra. If I succumbed, if I invited in the girly girl, I would be asking for that jackhammer. I did not want to be stung, not again.

So when she moved in close to my face, I hissed, "What are you doing?"

"Kissing you," she said and leaned into me again. This time our lips met, and I felt something entirely new. This was not just the soft shiver of a woman's lips. That was there, but there was something else, some stirring, some water main break deep within me. From inside I heard a cry, *Drop to your knees*.

I was shocked. I had never dropped to my knees. This was the first time a kiss told me to drop. I tried to push her away as she ran her square thumb over my lower lip, and her eyes flashed with squalid reflections of street lights. She kissed me again, and again I felt it. *Surrender.*

I went with her up into her apartment that night, but we did not make love. Angela passed out the moment she lay down, and I got dressed, ran back out into the wet parking lot, terrified that Marie would come home and find me naked in her bed. All the way home I slapped myself on the head. *Dumbshit. Stupid. What were you doing there? She's not even your type.*

Yet the next day when Angela came by to apologize, we smoked a joint and kissed again, and again inside, I dropped to my knees. *Oh, keep kissing me.* Something between my hips had broke open, and I'd never felt so hot down there before.

Naked together on my futon she ran her wide hands along my narrow frame. "You're shaped like a snake," she said, and that hurt me. I didn't mind if I wasn't as pretty as her others, but a snake? Who'd want to kiss a snake? I frowned, and she kissed me again, while she slipped one finger into my cunt. "I didn't mean it bad," she said.

Her mouth on one nipple, she sucked until it stung me, and with her free hand she kneaded the other nipple to a point. The finger in me circled deep, pressed into the bulb of my cervix. The sharp waves hurt a little, but I wanted more, the opening walls of me sucking her deeper. She slipped out again, rubbed my blood-filled clit. The longer she stroked, the more my body filled up with itself, a basin overflowing with hot, hot water. I came without noise, except for the roaring, the wild water rushing between my ears.

That was the first time I had an orgasm without watching

myself do it. Not even Irena, who I loved so much, could do that for me. All it took was a touch of that wide thumb, and the ghost of my usual self rose to my throat shivering.

It was the way she was in her body that made me fall in love with Angela, that loose-in-her-skin, boy-on-a-skateboard ease. In bed I fell to her, laid down flat on my back and opened my legs as far as they would widen, but she never stung me. She made me feel beautiful, like a beautiful girl in a yellow-beaded bra, and I liked it. I liked being her girly girl.

Then I flipped her over and she fell to me, not girlish, but bashful, embarrassed to be on her back, like it was unnatural but she'd do it, just for me, her cunt reddening, wanting my fingers, my mouth.

Then she flipped me back over again. When I came, I heard a small voice in the back of my throat whispering, *This is me, this is me, this is me.*

burning down the house

I hate my job. That's the first thing. I wait tables at the American Legion and I hate the drunks in crew cuts who come in after Vikings' games and never tip. I hate the blond women in high-heeled sandals who drink margaritas and flirt with the mean old vets. I especially hate the wall hangings, framed fragments of wind-ripped American flags. But that's not all. Rattling toward home in the back of the bus, the walls of my throat feel thick. This is when the story begins, when I admit it. Something is wrong with my body. It must be the cheap restaurant tea, I think, or the cigarettes.

I started smoking again at this job. There's nothing else to do with my hands when I sit in the break room with Madeline, a six-foot-tall old-timer with a platinum beehive. Madeline tells me she thinks Ronald Reagan is a wonderful man and Geraldine Ferraro should stay home and take care of her kids. I have been afraid of all the old-time waitresses I've ever worked with, ever since my first day in the Norse Room at the Leamington Hotel. The gnarled headwaitress made me cry when she accused me of turning up the toast machine, burning all her customers' toast. Madeline looks capable of making me cry. When she talks to me, I smoke.

The lunch bartender has a crush on me. Every afternoon

on my way out he gives me a triple vodka tonic in a foam cup. On the bus I sip, then hold the vodka and the tinny-tasting tonic still in my mouth before I swallow.

When I am alone I look at my body in the mirror, touch the image of my face, see a filmy shape, a muddled shadow.

I have a lover, Angela. In bed, before we touch, we toke up until we're high enough to feel the space between our naked bodies. Then Angela touches me and my body lights up, a lantern wick, tremulous blue and gold.

Even though she lives with another woman. Even though she never sleeps through the night with me. Even though she has passed out drunk in bed with me three or four times in the course of our affair. Even though she telephones me drunk, in the middle of the night, to tell me she still feels me on her fingers. Even though I hear her other lover in the background, whimpering, lifting a glass of ice tea or scotch, the ice cubes chiming.

I am skinny. That's what Grandma tells me when I am three or four, long before the start of this story.

You're so skinny you're gonna dry up and blow away.

I am unraveling in the wind. Flecks of myself are unreeling, a skinny tornado of unbound thread. Grandma keeps snakes in the basement, Grandpa says. He is Mommy's father. Every day I stay here while Mommy is at work. Grandpa's breath is stinky, his talk all blurry. He sits me in his lap, bumps me on his pokey knee. He rubs his prickly white whiskers against my cheek. He whispers, *Grandma makes meatloaf out of those snakes.*

They announced it on the radio, a tornado warning. In the story I'm having one of my hormone-crazy days, wild with sadness. This is how they say women are supposed to get when they're pregnant, but I know there aren't any babies in me. Sirens throb, clouds punch across the sky, and I live alone in a second-story apartment. I know today I'm going to die.

Earlier this afternoon I watched while my two best friends had a fight so horrible that one told the other she wanted to kill her. My friends, they've gone too crazy to save me. And Angela, she won't come. She's probably making love to the other one right now. Later she'll want to tell me how great sex is during a tornado. On the radio they say I should take cover under a heavy piece of furniture. I tip over a cushioned chair, balance it over my back, press the boom box, tuned to the weather channel, into my stomach. Outside the air is still and humid and dark, and inside I am crying.

At worst there is the pain, white noise in my belly.

Pain that bleaches my mind, bleaches my vision, sets the room undulating around me as I grip the slippery porcelain surface of the sink, retch into the toilet.

Friends tap on the door, but I tell them to go. My world bleaches another shade whiter. I pass out.

Grandpa's always drunk. Except today. A Saturday, years before the story begins. He takes me to Calumet Park, on the East Side, the far south corner of Chicago's lakeshore.

Mom and Dad both grew up around here. Now we live a few miles south, in the suburbs. We come up here a lot, to see Grandma and Grandpa, to eat at the Golden Shell where they play Croatian music on Fridays.

Today it showers, sharp pinpricks of rain that bite when they hit my face. The sky is dark, and the lake wipes its gray hands on the dirty beach. We walk. We don't touch. The thought of his touch makes me shiver, makes goose bumps rise on my neck. We don't talk. I'm not even sure this is really happening.

The windows and doors of the park buildings are boarded. They look like torn faces, bandaged mouths and eyes. The beach is littered with cigarette butts, pop-eyed dead fish, a treasure of concrete rubble and crushed Coke bottles.

Grandpa's skin looks yellow. Does he have blood? His face is stubbled with rough gray hairs. His voice always slurs. He's scary today, like all the other days, but I guess he's not drunk because there's no yelling. Not like usual. Not like last Christmas when he sat on the living room floor and would not get up. It took both my uncles to yank him to his feet, drag him, stumbling, to the car. Today there is no yelling. There is only the sound of water rising and falling, the sound of rubble knocking against itself, the hoarse sound of a dead man's breathing.

The story is over and I have not had a drink for more than four years, but tonight I am drunk.

I reel on my back porch, pour vodka into my macrobiotic tea. When my sickness happened I stopped drinking. Now I am better. I am better and now I want to be drunk. Janis Joplin is singing on the radio. Her voice growls, and I cry.

Grandpa died from this I think, but tonight Grandpa is alive. I feel his horsey breath seeping out my pores. Drunk, I am dead and Grandpa is alive, living in my body. I want to tear off my skin, tear him out of me. I reel and slip more vodka into my tea.

The Doctor in this story says I have Colitis.

The Doctor says I have Dysentery, or is it Typhoid? He asks if I have recently been to India.

The Doctor says I have Pelvic Inflammatory Disease.

The Doctor says I have Hypoglycemia.

The Doctor says I have a Cyst the size of a grapefruit.

The Doctor says I have a Yeast Infection in all the organs of my body.

The Doctor says if I don't take his two-hundred-dollar-a-bottle hormones the Cyst will bore through my intestinal walls and I'll have to shit in a bag.

The Doctor emerges from between my legs, looks down at the *People* magazine open on the floor, featuring photos of Princess Stephanie in a bikini.

The Doctor says, *Ooh, that's some swimsuit.*

When we get to the part of the story where Angela leaves me she says, *You aren't the woman I fell in love with.*

She's right. When I got sick I became my own double, two selves fighting for one body.

Pain every day is different from incidental pain. The first signs are shrill, a high familiar tone, a mourner's song.

My pain gathers in a narrow stream, sand through a funnel. It pulls me into a dry whirlpool of everything I've ever hated in myself.

Angela is right. There are two of me. Only one of us is alive.

Our dog Charro is my friend, even though he bites everyone in our family. I am thirteen, and a decade will pass before the story begins.

We've always had big dogs. The first one, Toro, was a shepherd collie that my mom adopted when my dad was in the service. Toro hated all of us children. Once he jumped up on my best friend and bit her on the ear. When he was old he had hip dysplasia. We put him to sleep. Now we have a German shepherd,

Charro.

Charro isn't fixed. He likes to sneak out the back door and sniff around in the nearby yards, terrorizing the neighborhood schnauzers. The first few times we caught him by the collar and pulled him home. Then my dad took him down into the basement and whipped him with a leash. His yelps rose through the kitchen linoleum.

So now whenever we try to nab him, he bites. He's always sorry afterward. He licks our wounds, hangs his head, creeps home. I have the second most scars in the family, on my wrists and fingers. My mother has the most, but she started earlier. She had to live with Grandpa.

An endometrial cyst on my right ovary the size of a grapefruit. A systemic yeast infection, opportunistic, because my immune system is weak. I had one of these cysts before this story, on my left ovary. Four years earlier, when I was just twenty-one, the doctor split open my abdomen, pulled out the cyst and the ovary. This new doctor puts me on birth control pills. Suppression Therapy. It's called that because it suppresses the menstrual cycle.

The pills make me so depressed my eyes are wide and pale. I can barely control the urge to rip the skin off my chest. I hurl a pen at my ex-lover Irena. We're having an argument one humid afternoon in the office in the back of an anarchist bookstore where we are arts administrators. Throwing a pen is not the most violent thing I can think of to do, but it startles me. I never get angry.

Irena leaves, and I can't stop crying. When she comes back I'm still crying and she doesn't know what to do, so she offers to buy me a puppy.

A few years before the story, when I am a freshman in college, my strongest belief is that time is an arbitrary invention. That's why I'm trying something new, twenty-four hours awake and twelve hours asleep.

The other thing is food. When I still lived at home, Mom made me eat all kinds of stuff I hated—pork chops, meatloaf, steak. Now I skip the gross dorm meals. If I eat, I eat pizza by the slice, inch-thick crust and really cheesy, or beef and bean tacos from Pepito's, or Wendy's burgers with extra sauce that runs down my hands when I bite in.

I need coffee, about two pots a day. I like it black and so strong it stings. Some days I can go on just coffee and an ice-cream sandwich from the vending machine.

My favorite drink is vodka and amaretto, so sweet I can't tell I'm getting drunk. I don't do rum and Coke anymore since that night I can't remember when I threw up all over my roommate's bed. But pot is what I like the best. I'll eat anything if I've had a joint first.

I'm never sick, unless I'm hungover. Last month I had the most bizarre hangover. It lasted a week. Then I was sick for a while first semester. I couldn't get out of bed, not even to take my finals. The health service told me I was anemic, and I was relieved it was such a dumb little thing. The only thing I get real bad are colds. If I start coughing in winter it lasts until the snow melts. But then I tell people I have consumption, like those beautiful, sickly girls in Russian novels. Sometimes they look at me strangely, and I think maybe they believe me.

I read a magazine story about a woman who the doctors said needed surgery, a total hysterectomy and hormone pills for the rest of her life. *You're not the woman I married,* her husband told her. She tried macrobiotics, and in a year her cysts had vanished. Now she works construction, twelve hours a day, says she's never been happier.

Why can't I be one of the healed? I don't want my belly split open again. I don't want to take those hormone pills that make me feel so crazy and sad. The doctors in my story don't believe me when I tell them about my headaches, my bleached patches of exhaustion, the bleary tingle behind my eyes that warns me I'm moving into one of the bad times.

I take out a loan to see a Naturopath, a Homeopath, a Chiropractor, and a Macrobiotic Cooking Instructor.

Still, I am losing weight. Still, the cyst is growing—some unwanted, mutant fetus.

I missed the commuter train from the Loop. I have to wait an hour for the next one.

It's my parents' Silver Anniversary, just a bit before the story. My Uncle Joe picks me up from the station. We discuss the Nicaraguan Revolution until I realize he thinks revolutionaries are criminals. I stop speaking. I am a radical lesbian-feminist. I am adamant about this. I refuse to pay for haircuts or buy dress-up clothes. All I have to wear to this party are white muslin trousers, cut too close in the crotch, and a shirt I got from the Salvation Army store—made of patterned terry with loose elastic in the waistband.

My Aunt Lucy's house is decorated with streamers and silver foil. I drink wine and boast to Uncle Luke, who has been a car mechanic his whole life, how another woman and I took apart the engine of a Pinto. The Pinto used to be his car. I make it sound like he was the one who screwed up the engine in the first place. I make it sound like I think I'm so smart I could learn everything in the world he knows by reading just one book. I don't mention that I hated how the grease felt in the creases of my palms, how my friend Debby had talked me into it, Debby with the astonishing red hair and all the dope I could ever hope to smoke. My uncle fidgets while I talk. I drink more wine.

Later I go out to the yard to smoke a cigarette. I notice the hedge looks like it's wiggling. It looks like a wiggling snake. Then I am on my knees, my body wracked with heaving. My lips spatter bitter phlegm. I am drunk. I am stupid drunk. When I am done throwing up I sit on the grass and smoke my cigarette. I see my grandma's shadow watching from the kitchen doorway.

I am feeling better, or I never would have let Dina into this story.

Dina woos me by showing me her paintings and playing me Frank Sinatra records. The paintings are cartoonish and tell me sad stories. I sit on the floor to look better, and my miniskirt hikes up higher on my hips. Dina stares at my legs which are thin now because there are so many things I can't eat. She tells me that David Hockney is her hero, but it's the novels of J.D. Salinger that inspire her. She looks up from my legs to my eyes. *Strangers in the night, exchanging glances* is what Frank is crooning, and I know I can't stand to do anything but go to bed with her.

Most days now I am not in pain. The bleached feeling comes and goes, but I've quit drinking, quit smoking pot and cigarettes. I've quit sugar, eat only whole grains and vegetables. I no longer come home dizzy and crying.

But I still have the shits every day, and I'm even more skinny than before. Every day someone new says *God, you're too skinny,* but I like my body this way, except the bleary spells, except how it hurts when Dina lays on top of me, on my stomach.

Last night, after a party at her house, we lay naked in her

bed and she fed me leftover noodles with peanut sauce. I am better. I can eat what I want. Today my gut aches.

This morning I tell her we have to get more sleep. On these mornings after all-night sex a gray mist engulfs me. I can't remember names or numbers. My abdomen curls and flexes, a fist, then not a fist. *It's been sweet that we can't get any sleep,* Dina says. *And romantic. Now you want to end it.*

It's worse. The pain is worse. I'm skinnier than before. Dina hates me for this. Her little brother just killed himself with a heroin overdose, and he was the same age as me. When she looks at my face, my heavy-lidded eyes, something infuriates her. Maybe she sees her dead brother looking back.

Pain is with me like my skin, like my fingernails, like the ridges in my mouth. It's heavy, a cold weight dropping and dropping, fueling itself with everything wet in me.

I have always felt like a loose wire sparking.

In this photograph, taken just months before the story, my family sits on the front porch of my parents' house. It's Christmas, but oddly warm for Chicago in December. We do not wear coats. We are all there: me, my father, my mother, Paulie and Benny, my brothers. I am the strange one, the queer one, the only one to leave the family, leave Chicago. We do not speak of this. My father sets the camera on automatic. No one touches. We all smile vaguely. Everyone is encased, their own silent wire. The dog and I are set off from the rest. I appear to be laughing, or grimacing. The dog appears to be whispering to me. *Get away. Why did you return? Slip out before the shutter clicks and nothing you remember will be true.*

I am in pain in Dina's bed on a Saturday. She went to her studio to paint and now she is back. *The smell of your sickness fills up the whole house,* she tells me. *I don't mind,* she says, *but don't you think it's interesting?*

What she smells is not me. This we discover later. She smells the rice I cooked for my lunch and left sitting on the stove. On this day I hate her more than I hate the pain.

I wake up in Dina's bed with the pain in the middle of the night.

I make a hot water bottle. The skin on my stomach is turning grayish brown, stained from the burn of water bottles and heating pads.

Dina wakes, and we watch the late show together, the color version of *The Phantom of the Opera.* Claude Rains' face is disfigured by acid, and so the woman he loves is afraid of him. I wonder if Dina is afraid of me. We run our thighs together, and she falls asleep. Her warm breath settles on my bare neck. I turn to her, watch her breathe. I look down at myself. Who is this body? Whose neck is this catching her breath?

Am I dying? I don't cry at all. Dina calls me a corpse. I hate her for saying it, but not enough to get up, make a plan, figure out whether or not I'm dying. It's so quiet. There are no sirens.

These days, long after the story, I still think about Dina's paintings, how I'd like to see them again. I don't want to see Dina again, yet I am sitting across from her, in a living room of another of her ex-lovers. Dina moved to New York; now she is visiting. I didn't want to see her, but it seemed cruel to refuse. I agreed— for only two hours.

I found your letters, Dina is saying. *They're so sweet. It helped me remember there were good things about us.*

I remember good things, I say.

I understood who you were, Dina says. *I liked that.*

I don't agree, but I don't want to start an argument. I say, *I liked our sex. After Angela I was afraid I'd never have good sex again.*

All I remember was you were too sick for sex, she says.

No, we had great sex before I was too sick.

I never knew you except when you were sick. I didn't know you before. I haven't known you since.

We are silent, staring at each other across this unfamiliar coffee table, sitting on clean upholstered furniture much nicer than I am accustomed to. My back hurts. I didn't mean to admit that I liked anything about her. I am shocked by how familiar her face looks to me, exactly how she looked when she was my lover. Today the only pull I feel is away from her.

We were both at our worst, I say. *Me so sick, your brother dying.*

She says, *We had good talks about art.*

We were in it too long. It scares me, I say.

Only a year, she says, and shrugs. *Most do it for their whole lives.*

I have acupuncture every day. Alexander, the naturopath in this story, says I'm having a healing crisis, but now the cyst is protruding out past the usual lines of my abdomen, the size of a large, heavy softball, a sixteen-incher, the kind girls' teams used when I was a kid. Every session costs thirty dollars. My loan

is used up and I can't work. I can barely sit up in the car. I owe
the naturopath all this money. I owe everyone all this money.

So now this guy, this Alexander, tells me he's leaving town
to follow Halley's Comet.

I meet with his partner. She looks exactly like the actress
who played Loretta Hagers on "Mary Hartman, Mary Hartman."
I hate her boots. They're the kind women wore in the early
seventies, high to her knees with zippers up the back. She must
be stupid, I think, to wear those boots.

She asks me to describe my condition. I begin the story, again
this story, terse, belligerent words. I start to cry and I can't stop.
She says to me, *Put on your coat.*

We walk four times around a tiny park with a shallow lagoon
in its center. It's a good thing this is a day I am strong enough
to walk.

I tell her I never eat cheeseburgers or chocolate-chip cookies or cherry donuts or Coca-Cola or milk.

I don't drink St. Pauli Girl or Beck's dark on tap or Leinen-
kugel's cold in bottles. I don't drink Chablis or Lambrusco or
Schwarze Katz Liebfraumilch, or Tanqueray tonics or godmothers
or Schnapps.

I don't smoke Hawaiian or Columbian or Thai stick, or even
Salem Menthol Lights.

I soak rags in water boiled with ginger, press them into my
stomach until they leave red welts. I fill stainless steel pans with
water, alternately dip my hips into hot, into cold.

I swallow tiny effervescent pills that Alexander gave me after he looked up my symptoms in his old blue books that unravel
at the bindings.

Aaron, my chiropractor, cracks my neck at least three times
a week, and the pills, oh the vitamins. I swallow thirty every day.

And every day I lie still on a high metal table while Alexander heats the tips of the acupuncture needles. And every night

I stick slimy green paste up my vagina with a popsicle stick.

Still, I am in pain.

It's almost Easter. There's a little snow on the ground. The wind bites into our cheeks. She says, in her sweetest Loretta Hagers voice, *It sounds like you feel sad and deprived. If you need to break out and eat a chocolate bunny, then eat a choco-late bunny.*

Then, she says, *decide what you're going to do.*

Years after the story, I am trying to explain it to Jane, my alcoholism treatment counselor.

I hold my hands up in front of my face, two feet apart. *Over here is my alcohol and drug use,* I say, wiggling the left hand. *And this is my sickness,* I say, wiggling the right. *I get so con-fused,* I say, *trying to sort it out.*

What happens if you move the two together? Jane asks.

I shiver and drop my hands. She is staring at me, not even blinking. *You mean drinking made me sick?*

I don't want you to simplify, she says. *But add in marijuana and not eating.* Jane stops to hold up her hands, then counts these things off on her long fingers. *Your terror of your grand-father,* she continues. *And depression, not knowing your feel-ings, and don't forget all that coffee.* She lays her hands down in her lap to finish. *And your alcoholism,* she says.

I don't want to do this. I'm cold all over. I say, *I can't stand the thought of it.*

Why not? Jane says. She wears an expression, tender and attentive, that makes me feel great love for her. Sometimes she reminds me of my father, because she's smart and laughs at my jokes. Except my father doesn't pay attention to me like this. I wish I were her baby, curled up in her lap. I wish I could wail, *Love me, love me,* until she stroked my brow and kissed my forehead.

So my body just couldn't take it? I ask. *So I drank too much, smoked too much pot, got too stressed out and my body just went haywire?*

What you think?

I shrug and say, *It could be true.*

Jane nods. I am embarrassed by how much I love her and now I am hot, my skin burning up. I have to turn my eyes away, and when I do I am cold again and back to not believing I can get through this.

On Fridays Rocky wears his special shirt. This week it's a red Hawaiian. It makes him look tan even though it's February.

I am lying on the table in his office. I hold my left arm straight up into the air as he presses points on my body and pulls down on my arm. This is called Applied Kinesiology. He calls his method Holographic Diagnosis, and I love the way that sounds, my body illuminated and three-dimensional on a slowly spinning screen.

I hate doctors, but I love Dr. Rocky Ciambrone. I came to him first just after the story ended. He's a chiropractor, but more than just a bone cracker. Rocky touches a point on my throat, and the strength in my upright arm gives out. He takes out a box filled with small vials of fluid. He places one on this same spot on my neck, but my arm is still weak. He chooses another, and still my arm is weak. He chooses a third and tries to pull down on my arm. This time my arm is strong again.

He says, *I'll give you some of this herb mixture. Take four drops a day for ten days.*

What is it for?

Your thyroid is weak, he says. *That's why you can't get rid of your cough. You should have an MD check it out, too.*

Once Rocky gave me pills that looked like tiny black pearls.
They made me throw up for an entire week, but afterward I was
free from a flu I'd had for two seasons. Every time it's some new
weird thing. Still, I do whatever he tells me to. He's different from
the others, the ones I saw before who refused to say they could
be wrong. Rocky has never asked me to follow only him. Cell by
cell my body rebuilds.

Your earrings, they're shaped like snakes, he says. *Why do
you like snakes?*

Snakes mean change, I tell him.

I've just started going to a group about snakes, Rocky says.
We're going to discover our own snakiness.

What does that mean? Can you have snakiness?

That's what I want to find out, he says.

I am visiting my family. The story is just beginning. I am not
drinking and so I notice. My father has a martini. My mother has
a glass of wine. My brother has a beer. We are getting ready to
go out to dinner, to the East Side, the Golden Shell—drinks,
chicken, three-bean salad, and a man with an accordion. As we
leave the house, my brother grabs another bottle of beer. My
mother pours herself another glass of wine. My father carries
his second martini, balances it on the dash, settles into the
driver's seat. I am alone here, a loose wire sparking. I notice, and
listen to all our breathing.

A new gynecologist gives me codeine. I get on Medical As-
sistance. This gynecologist is the only good MD in this story,
which means she is the only one I don't hate. I don't hate her,
so I love her. Together we decide I will have surgery.

The good gynecologist removes the cyst and rebuilds my remaining ovary with her fingers. My friends who wait report that she comes out of the operating room sweaty and disheveled. Later I joke to Dina that no woman has ever touched me so deeply.

For a week afterward I am shaking and sweating. I have a post-operative infection. My immune system still can't keep up. It was too much to hope that the surgery would solve everything. I wake every night, perspiration soaked through the hospital gown, through the sheets. A needle is stuck into a vein in my hand and attached to a bag of antibiotic fluid. If I move suddenly the machine beeps wildly, a grating noise that makes my incision ache.

Dina broke up with me two weeks ago, but she visits. We lie on the hospital bed together and watch *It's a Wonderful Life*. Then I drape my robe over my shoulder, drag the beeping machine that makes me feel part-automated, hold my free arm across my incision, and ride the elevator up to where they keep the new babies. One has a tiny green cap on her head. I watch the light rise and fall of her chest as she sleeps.

Rocky and I are quiet while he holds my skull in his palms, cracks the bones into place at the tip of my spine.

Even though my story ended, it never ends. I've become someone different, someone sick. So I say, *I'm so afraid I'll never be healthy.*

Don't you feel healthy? he asks.

The question stops me. I get bad colds and flus more often than most, yet something has changed. Am I sick now, or was it then, my whole life before the story that was my sickness? I do feel a throb of life in me that was missing, even as a child. I do feel a pumping of blood in me, the blood that was gone from Grandpa's face.

The story ends when I lie on my bed at St. Mary's Hospital. I am rescued, not recovered. Yet I know that when I leave here my life will be new. I am listening to a tape in my walkman, the Talking Head's song, ''Burning Down the House.'' When I close my eyes I see myself in a green dress, spinning and spinning, my chest rising and falling with breath, spinning and chanting, *My Life, My Life, My Life.*

miss south side of chicago

I'm not the daughter my parents wanted. They would have preferred Miss South Side of Chicago—a girl with a talent for ballet or baton and no talent for recognizing the family sadness. A blond beauty pageant winner. The family prize. The one who would carry them to better and better neighborhoods. The prettiest, most outgoing, football-loving white girl born south of 103rd and Torrence.

South is the direction my mother moved, once she married and left her home. She grew up in the South Dearing projects, three blocks from 103rd and Torrence, two blocks from Wisconsin Steel. At the turn of the century it was a steel mill neighborhood, practically its own little city. My grandfather worked for the sanitary district, in the plant that cleaned shit from the water supply, but most of the neighborhood men were steelworkers. Today the mills are pretty much vacant—rusted old frames and piles of copper-colored slag. Now mostly Blacks and Mexicans live there. "It's gotten bad," my family says.

Of the two sisters in her family, my mother is the smart one. Her name is Bebe, short for Beatrice, and she was pretty enough. Black-and-white photos of Bebe in her early twenties look like the calendar shots you see of Marilyn Monroe before she bleached her hair. But my mother didn't have time to be a beauty queen. She concentrated on putting herself through college, majoring in math and physical education, the only one in her family to go past high school. Her little sister, my Aunt Lucy, was taller, bigger-breasted, thin as a stick from her waist to her thighs, an expert at fixing her hair and applying eyeliner. She was a natural blond and could have been Miss South Side, but she concentrated on getting a job as a telephone operator when she finished high school, and then on getting married, and then on moving to a big house in California.

My mom, Aunt Lucy, me. We're all Miss South Side; none of us are Miss South Side. There's really no such thing. Every neighborhood has its royalty—Miss Stony Island, Miss Calumet Park, Miss Tulip Festival of South Holland—but there's no single queen to represent the whole thing. The mills. The paint factories. The dead terrain. The landfills. The sanitary district. The graffiti and rickety commuter lines. The old neighborhoods that white people say went bad when the colors changed. The boxy brick near South Side suburbs where I went to grade school. The small-but-sleek prefab split-levels a bit farther south where my parents live still, that I hear people say are going bad now too.

But Miss South Side is more than all this. She's a talkative white girl who chews gum and uses a curling iron to flip her blond bangs up off her forehead. A party girl who would hang by her ankles out a moving car to root for the Bears, the Bulls, the White Sox. A straight girl who fears the Blacks, the queers, all the unsavory characters that have taken over the old neighborhoods. She's good at math but better at gymnastics. She's surprisingly elegant in high-heeled pumps and a tight little dress in red or bright yellow. She laughs loud, talks rough, doesn't like to sit around. She's every businessman's favorite teller or waitress. She's the bright blond head wearing a silver crown that makes bad memories disappear. She's the one I could have been. She is nothing like me.

I try to love my family, even though I'm not what they wanted. Even though I worry they'll frown when they see me, my hair streaked auburn and copper, the color of the slag heaps, my clothes blousy cottons that I hope hides the thirty pounds my mother keeps begging me to lose. I leave my adult home, Minneapolis, to visit them one or two times a year. Sometimes my lover Linnea comes with me, but this time she's staying up north, in Waukegan with her family. I'm driving south to be with mine. I hit traffic on the southbound Edens.

Dad and Mom are on their second bottle of wine by the time I make it downtown. My brother Benny is sipping a Coke. The Greek Islands. Greek Town. My parents' favorite. I'm late, and Mom and Dad are annoyed.

"Nice you could make it," Mom says meanly. Dad's lips are stiff when he leans toward me to kiss my cheek.

My brother Benny says, "It's about time," in a whiny voice. "You've ruined my dinner." He's always had such an odd sense of humor. Who knows if he's serious.

Tonight I notice how much he looks like our dad—just as tall, the same wide, athletic shoulders, narrow waist and long thighs they get from dutiful jogging, that olive skin I've always thought of as the Croatian in us, and the same receding hairline, although Dad's hair is white now. And they have the same grin, the one that seems to say, *This is all so stupid.*

Next to them my mother seems like a miniature of herself. When I was a kid adults were always telling me that I was tall because my parents were tall, but now I see, my father is the tall one.

"You've ruined my dinner," Benny repeats.

"Shut up, Benny. You're not funny," I say, as my father orders another bottle of Roditis. The host is a stocky Greek man in a silver-gray suit with a sharp line and boxy shoulders. Linnea would look great in that suit, I think. He motions for us to follow him to a tiny table under a mural of a white sand shoreline.

Following my parents and Benny to the table I think about how I want to love my family, but I always feel so unrelated to them. I do feel our kinship—the shade of our skin, the shape of words in our mouths, the cut of our noses and chins—yet at the same time I feel like a child of a different country, a different culture, with a different set of rules that I use to understand the world. I want to know all the secrets and hidden truths of things. They say there aren't any.

My youngest brother Paulie is not here tonight. He's on a vacation in Europe with his girlfriend Mitsuko, a travel agent who gets them great deals on airline tickets. Paulie is the only one in my family who's ever asked me questions about my life. *Are your friends gay too? Do you tell people or do you try to hide it?* He's the only one who looks at me without seeing everything I'm not. Sometimes he's even the interpreter between the rest of the family and me.

I wish Paulie were here with Mitsuko, a dark woman, native Japanese, with a narrow waist, skinny wrists and ankles, a size three. My whole family towers over her. Ever since Paulie went to Japan with Mitsuko, he seems to understand that the world is full of people who are not our family. When Mitsuko comes to dinner, she and I are the foreigners, the football-haters, laughing at my family's boundless talk about sports teams, sports players, sports scores. Alone with my parents and Benny, I don't know who I am. I try to pose as Miss South Side of Chicago.

I've never wanted to be Miss South Side. I've always wanted to be Miss South Side.

Miss South Side of Chicago has hair blond as a lit bulb. My hair was ash blond when I was girl, but it streaked white blond in the summer months.

Miss South Side's red fingernails are as long as the beaks of woodpeckers. I've never been able to grow out my nails and when I try to paint them, I get nail polish all over my clothes and the furniture.

When she takes the time to dress up, the evening light shimmers off Miss South Side's hose. I can't wear pantyhose without ruining them. It touches my skin and automatically runs, like a body rejecting a donated kidney. What I can wear is fishnets and black leather miniskirts. *What a slut,* Miss South Side of Chicago would say.

Miss South Side spends her free time in supper clubs where they serve prime rib and Bordeaux. On special nights she wears her hair swept up on her head like a tornado, her bangs feathered back above her ears. She sits on a leather upholstered stool at the supper club bar—Geno's in Harvey, or any of the dozens along the wide Western Avenue strip. The bartenders know her name. I drank quietly, in darker spots, narrow as hallways with pool tables squeezed into the back, or gay discos with mirror balls that reflected the faces of a hundred other drunks in the corners of my smudged glasses.

Miss South Side waits for a good-looking white guy to pick up the bill, sipping her tonic with gin, hair as blond as the yellow light at the edge of a candle's flame. I gulped gin and tonics too, and there was a time that I left with men, once even an upholstery salesman. But I turned out to be the type who'd rather marry a woman. *Miss South Side gags at the thought of lezzies. Her face scrunches up like a used tissue, and she looks like she might have to spit.*

The restaurant is packed, wall to wall. Groups of people squeeze around tables too small to hold them: some of them Greek families, some of them packs of young white straight couples drunk on Roditis and beer, some romantic twosomes, a man and a woman sharing wine. In Chicago there are more black people than in Minnesota, but in Minneapolis you see more inter-

racial couples. Here, at least on the South Side, the couples hud-
dling over candles, wineglasses touching, are always both dark-
skinned or both white. If big blond Paulie were here with Mitsuko people wouldn't exactly stare, not the way they would gape
if his lover were a black woman. Still, you'd be able to see it in
their eyes, the uneasiness, the taking note.

My lover Linnea is an obvious lesbian in her tailored men's
clothes and long gait. If we were here in this restaurant, just the
two of us, people would stare. The last time I walked down a busy
street in Chicago with Linnea, we were on our way to a sushi
bar on the near North Side. It wasn't even the South Side where
I would have thought to be scared. It was New Town, the gayest
part of the city. I was wearing a leather miniskirt, and she was
wearing leather pants. We weren't holding hands, not even
touching shoulders, when two big white men wearing sweatpants and athletic shoes shoved by us close enough that we could
smell the beer on their breath. The big blond one leaned into
my face and shouted, "You're scaring me—GET AN EXORCIST."
Maybe I would have to be Miss South Side if I still lived here.

The restaurant smells of smoke, garlic, and cheese. The tables are close enough together that I can smell the wine on the
breath of the woman with long bleached hair and thick red lipstick, wearing a tight little red dress, sitting sideways in her chair
at the table next to us. There she is, a real Miss South Side. I examine her, try to see what is the same about us. We're both tall,
but she's thirty pounds lighter. Her nose is a little too long to be
WASP, so she's probably Eastern European stock, like me. I try
to picture her with shorter hair, dyed auburn, one long purple
earring, hiking boots, a loose-fitting, dark pink denim jumpsuit.
Would she look like me? She's sitting with a group of men and
women. They all look to be in their early thirties. I can't tell if
one of the men is her date. They're all noisy and drinking a lot.
She laughs, a little too loud, the timbre of her voice ragged
around the edges. Her chair is set off from the table, just an inch

or two, so I think that even though she looks the talkative type, maybe, like me, she is the one who watches.

I turn my long-stemmed glass over onto its rim so the waiter, or my mother, can't tempt me by filling my glass with wine. I'm a recovering drunk, but I haven't exactly told my parents this. They know I used to drink and now I don't. My parents and Benny have never asked me why.

Benny sips a glass of wine, but just one. He's the only one in my family who's never drank much. He's always been that way. When we were kids he would horde chocolate on the shelf above his bed, taking one bite each day for a week, while Paulie, the youngest, and me, the oldest, swallowed whole candy bars, washed them down with Coke, and laughed at Benny.

The ones who are already drunk at the table next to us yell *Opaa! Opaa!* when a *saganacki*—flaming cheese—is lit anywhere in the dining room. We eat *saganacki* too, and *taramosalata*—fish roe pâté—while my parents drink their Roditis and argue with Benny about the University of Illinois coaching staff. God, I'm just here for three days, I think. I want to talk about something real.

When I say, "I dreamt about Grandpa Luschak last night," my mother's face wrinkles up like a fig.

"I dreamt he was still alive," I say, and our table is the only quiet one here.

"Damned Mexicans," Grandpa Luschak yelled. He was alive then, but he looked dead to me.

I rolled socks with Grandma in the living room of the second-story brick duplex apartment that overlooked Bensley Avenue, a block from the project apartment where my mom grew up. Little round Grandma, her hair thin but still brown then, rolled my grandfather's socks, black or gray, a thin-ribbed cotton-and-wool blend. We watched Lawrence Welk on the TV, and I helped her, holding the socks together toe to toe, rolling them up like little sleeping bags, turning the ankle end down, stuffing the toes into the pocket it formed. We made little balls of Grandpa's socks, tossed them together into the laundry basket.

Aunt Lucy was in her bedroom, her head under her own private stand-alone hair dryer, the kind they have at the beauty parlor, and Grandpa was yelling.

"Peggy, you Polack, where's my pants," screeching in his blurry voice. "Some damn Mexican must have stolen my pants."

Grandpa was crazy. There were Mexicans outside on their block but none in their apartment. Grandma's name wasn't Peggy. It was Josephine. Grandma said he changed it because Peggy was easier to say. I didn't understand why he couldn't just call her Josie. He drank whiskey while we rolled his socks. Aunt Lucy stayed in her room, sitting under her stand-alone hairdryer that must have cost weeks of what she made at the telephone company. Later she would twist her hair up on the top of her head like a caramel roll, as beautiful as a pageant queen. Until then she sat in the low hot rush of hair dryer air, while Grandma and I pretended the only noise was the boy on TV with the big teeth, smiling and pumping away on his accordion while the old couples with white paper-colored skin held each other and danced real slow.

We saw two black men dancing on the corner. "Quick, lock the car door," my mother said.

We were riding back into her old neighborhood. Grandma and Grandpa didn't drive, so we had to pick them up when they came to dinner. I spent the ride there planning ways to avoid riding in back with Grandpa on the drive home.

Through a slightly orange dusk, at the edge of the neighborhood, we saw a clump of black guys on the street corner. Two of them—one the color of fudge, the other light, no darker than

I am with a tan—swayed slow to music that poured from a radio the darker guy balanced on his shoulder. *Cause I'm eeeeeasy. Easy like Sunday morning.* They didn't touch, yet they were in sync, slow dancing, together, loose-limbed, their eyes closed. They didn't look at us.

Mom didn't say why we had to lock the doors. What was she afraid they would do? Were these the unsavory characters she always worried about? I looked out at the men and everything about Blacks I'd ever heard sped through my mind. Bad hair. They all look alike. *Eenie, Meenie, Miney, Moe. Catch a nigger by the toe.* We weren't allowed to say that word in our house. My mom said prejudice was wrong. So why did she reach over me, press down the button on my side of the car, and warn me, "Always lock your car door"?

"Why did you dream that?" Mom asks.

Her face is still wrinkled; her wine glass is suspended in the air over her plate. She seems to be considering. Could it be true? Could her father show up here?

"I don't know why," I say. "Maybe it was just because I was always scared of him."

"Scared of him?" Mom's face wrinkles up even more. "You couldn't be. He was such a sweet man." My father is smiling his this-is-so-stupid smile. Benny smiles too and shakes his head at me.

I'm not posing very well. Miss South Side would have never brought this up. I look over at Benny shaking his head at me, a sick half-smile on his face, as if I'd insulted my parents and he couldn't believe I had the gall. Miss South Side would have known that this was not acceptable dinner conversation. But shouldn't families talk to one another? Shovel through the past together? Get better and better at knowing what to do next?

I look to Miss South Side at the table next to me. Her mascara is smudged just below her right eye. She knows what to do next. She drinks her wine, holding the glass to her lips and letting the five, six, seven gulps slide down fast. She is the one who drinks for the feeling it gives her. I could be her. I watch the slight muscle bulge in her neck as she swallows and I can almost taste her wine going down.

"Of course I was scared of him, Mom. He was drunk all the time."

"Oh, now," she says, setting her glass back down on the table, "you just think that because that's what we always said about him."

I dream of the taste of wine. I dream of Grandpa Luschak.

In my dream he is stumbling along the icy sidewalk in Calumet City. My aunts and uncles help him to the door of a yellow brick house with a wrought-iron railing where we meet for his funeral. Inside, relatives sit in the living room on furniture stiff and sticky from the plastic protective covers. The mirror over the sofa holds the rising smoke of cigarettes.

We have paper plates of dinner on our laps—bean salad, Jello with fruit cocktail suspended inside it, sliced ham, and white rolls. The aunts are talking about the neighborhood, the Blacks moving in. They're scared, they say. They might sell, move further south. *Just don't sell to Blacks,* one of them warns.

My second cousin Katerine stands in the wood frame of the bedroom door, rubbing her stomach. She's the one who looks like me, the same face, except she has a perm in her hair and she's pregnant. Mrs. South Side of Chicago. Katerine refuses the Jello. *Makes my stomach twirl.*

I dream I am guzzling wine from a long-necked bottle as they seat Grandpa in a soft chair in the corner. They set his yellow, cigarette-stained hands on the cane balanced in front of his feet. They prop a pleated gray pillow, made by my Aunt Sis, behind his neck, to make him look more alive. I want to cover his face with a blanket. I want to smother him with the pleated gray pillow before he starts breathing, starts moving those fingers toward me.

My mom's cousin, a thick-waisted woman in a yellow dress and apron, pours coffee into my mother's cup with matching saucer. *Coffee, Bebe?*

As I sleep my tongue feels rubbery and dead.

As I dream my throat aches for more wine.

Grandpa's wrinkled head falls to one side.

My mom cradles her coffee cup in her open palms. *My dad was really sweet. My dad was a terrible man.*

"It was a relief when my dad died," Mom says.

"What a thing to say, Bebe," my father says.

"No, I mean it. It was a relief to my mother." Mom is drunk. She seems to be mostly talking to herself.

"He was a terrible man," she says, filling up her wineglass again.

I am holding my breath. I always knew there was a secret. Is Mom finally going to lift the lid? What is it? I know, but I'm afraid to think it. What will happen if she says it? I imagine the four of us springing into yellow flame like a whole platter of *saganacki*. I notice Mom's eyes are a little puffy.

"That's all I'm going to say," she says. "He was just awful, that's all. I won't say anything more." She is crying now. When I look close I can spot something. What is it? I want so bad for her to say it. I feel my whole life pushing out from inside me, hard against my cheeks and temples. What is it?

The walls of my throat squeezed together too tight when Grandpa reached his fingers toward me. My whole body pushed against the inside of my cheekbones. I had to get out of myself. "Watch out for them," he whispered. His fingers shook. Grandpa loved to touch my blond hair with his yellow cigarette-stained fingers. "Watch out for those Mexicans, Bebe," he coughed. His voice was bristly and his breath was full of whiskey. *There's no Mexicans here Grandpa*, I wanted to scream. "You're my little queen. Watch out for those *niggers*, my little Queen Bebe." *There's no one here but you, Grandpa. My name isn't Bebe, Grandpa. Bebe is my mom. There's no one here but you.* I wanted to scream and scream at him, but I couldn't. I couldn't do it. My throat was closed in on itself. I kept my screams a secret.

A thin, dark waiter slips our dinner plates in front of us. "What I want to know is how did he die," my father says. "There's a mystery there."

"Mystery?" The cheering and hooting from the next table makes it a little hard for me to hear. Miss South Side is hooting too, but she's starting to look a little sleepy. The corners of her lips are drooping, and the wine has worn away most of her lipstick.

"He passed out on the El," my mother says. "That's why they brought him to the hospital."

"He blacked out on the El?" It couldn't have been the only time he was drunk on the train.

"He passed out," my father corrects. "They took him to the hospital to see what was wrong."

"And whatever was wrong, he died of it?"

"No, they didn't find anything. He was supposed to be released the next day," he says.

"They called my mother the day she was supposed to come get him and said her husband was dead," Mom says. "Can you imagine?"

"They said he died of heart failure," Dad says. "All of a sudden, heart failure. There's a mystery there. I've always wanted to get to the bottom of it."

But we all know he died of drinking. What does this matter—the hospital, the mystery?

"Still, it was a relief to my mother." Mom is starting to cry again. Dad looks annoyed. Benny is sort of nodding at my father like a doll on a car dashboard. *Go on, come on, go on.* I'm tempted to let Dad take over now. He and Benny like to talk about their ideas of things. Will the Democrats ever win another presidential race? Should South Side white ethnics support Jesse Jackson? Did Grandpa's doctors have something to hide? Usually I'm relieved at this line of discussion. My father, an old-line but wavering Democrat, versus my brother, a new-liner, a devoted Republican-hater. It's interesting. It's not sports. Sometimes I even join in, even though they both see me as an over-the-line radical. But tonight my mother has led us to the locked box where the reason for a million things I've ever felt or done might be hiding. I don't want them to shut her up.

"How did he keep his job all those years?" I ask my mom.

Dad answers. "He didn't. He was fired from a few different mills."

I'd never heard that Grandpa was a millworker. But it made sense. Everyone in that neighborhood worked in the mills back then. "But wasn't he still working at the Sanitary District when he died?"

My mom is laughing a little, even though she's crying. "The guys he worked with used to lock him in his locker when he was too drunk to work, so he wouldn't get caught."

"None of you ever told on him," my father said, and now his voice is speeded up, the heavy *d*'s and *t*'s, the long vowels of his South Side accent more noticeable. "You never told, so he just kept on doing it."

I can't remember the last time I saw my dad get emotional. What will he do? Throw the table over on its side? Squeeze his wineglass until it shatters? But I'm mad, too. Why do I have to cause a big scene just to find out a little about who my family is? Why don't I already know these things? If I was the kind of daughter they wanted, would they have confided in me? I look over to Miss South Side to see if she's listening. She's drunk, slouched a little sideways in her chair, waving her arm in front of her, making some incoherent point that no one is listening to. Miss South Side doesn't care. That's the point. I'm not supposed to care. Miss South Side would rather talk about the game.

"You don't know the half of it," Mom says. "In this day and age he wouldn't get away with the things he did."

There are photos of those days, Grandpa alive, still some hope I would turn out different. One is from the day I was in my Aunt Lucy's wedding. Aunt Lucy is standing in the church foyer in her handmade white veil and her white lace and satin wedding dress, cut fashionably narrow from her waist to her ankles. Her hair is piled up in thick caramel loops on the top of her head, and her veil has a single satin rose that she wears pinned at the line of her bangs. I am the flower girl. I hold a white wicker basket full of pink carnations, and the dress I have on is pale pink, the same thick, shiny satin the bridesmaids' dresses are cut from. On my head is a rose folded in satin, just like Aunt Lucy's, but smaller. Pink net falls over my face, but I can't see my face in this photo. What I see is the back of my head, tilted up, one long banana curl trailing down my back.

My hair was fixed at the beauty parlor by Sandy, my mother's hairdresser. I sat under a stand-alone hair dryer and looked at movie magazines, all the beautiful movie stars with red-painted fingernails who wore their hair looped on the top of their heads. I sat in a gold-flecked chair as Sandy's soft fingers rolled my hair into long sausages and pinned them to the top of my head, while she chatted with the hairdresser next to her about how scary her neighborhood was getting now that the Blacks had started moving in. Sandy left one long strand loose at the nape of my neck to curl down my back. "There you are, Missy," she said when she was done. "A regular beauty queen."

In the foyer of the church my head is tilted up. My single loose curl grazes my waist. I am looking at Aunt Lucy's face. Her eyes are closed. Her father, my grandpa, is kissing her cheek. Aunt Lucy looks ecstatic, her moment of becoming, the moment of her release. Grandpa looks pale, pasty, as if he's been carried here, to Aunt Lucy's side, and someone lifted his chin up, poked him until his lips smacked against her cheek. My chin is tilted up. I am watching. Grandpa looks as if he's already dead. I'm watching to see how Aunt Lucy escapes.

Driving Grandma home from my parents house these days, I am still afraid of him, even though he is fifteen years dead. On 103rd, coming off the freeway, the land for miles around is barren and strewn with garbage. Driving this stretch I always find myself thinking that the world is nothing. There's nothing to believe in. I relax a little as we roll over the hill into rows of yellow apartment buildings and square, orange brick houses with picture windows and wrought-iron railings. "Is your door locked?" Grandma asks me as we turn onto Bensley Avenue. I had just been wondering if she is less afraid, now that Grandpa is so long dead. A couple of teenage Mexican boys cross the street in front of the car. They laugh and shout to each other in Spanish. One of them is bouncing a basketball. The other has a little stubble of dark beard on his chin, and I wonder if his facial hair has just started to grow.

"What are you afraid of Grandma?" I ask her.

"Oh, it's gotten bad around here," she says.

Finally my mother says it. "He made passes at me."

"Oh God, see what you started?" Benny says to me.

What I started? I didn't start it. I wish Paulie were here to defend me. But if Mitsuko had been here, my mom wouldn't have said a word. I wouldn't have been so bored, and I wouldn't have even mentioned Grandpa. It wouldn't have happened if Linnea were here either. I had to be alone with them, undefended, for this story to come out.

I stare at Benny, angry at first. But when I look in his eyes I see that the light in them is too bright. Maybe he is afraid of this story, afraid that my father will squeeze a wine glass to pieces, that my mother will cry and lay her head down in her dinner, that we will attract attention, that people will notice us. I wonder if for all these reasons he is afraid of me too, and so for a moment I am sorry again that I am not who I'm supposed to be.

"He took off all his clothes and made passes at me," Mom goes on. A *saganacki* is lit at a table behind us, and the people there yell *Opaa!*

We are all quiet for a minute. I stuff a few mouthfuls of spinach pie into my mouth, and for a moment I am distracted by the sweet spread of the garlic rising into my nose. I could stop this now. Should I? "How old were you?" I finally ask.

"High school age. And you know, it was particularly bad for me because I never did any of those things." Her words are just a little bit slurred.

"He did this a lot?"

"He did it enough. But I got out of there. I escaped."

Dad isn't eating. He's looking far off into the distance toward the large mural of a beachfront cafe on the far wall of the restaurant. He's grinning a sick grin again. I'm afraid I've pushed this too far. But I can't stop.

I look over to Miss South Side. I see she is mumbling and nearly passed out. She can't hold her head up straight, and two

of the men from her table are trying to hoist her out of her chair.
I have an urge to rush over to her, tell her what I know about
how to escape, but her chin falls down onto her chest. I see the
dark blond roots of her hair. As one hand falls loose to her side,
I notice her long fingernails are painted dark red, almost purple today.

"Mom," I say, "did you ever tell anyone?"

"Oh no."

Dad snaps awake at this. "You told me," he says. He's still
grinning, and his voice is jagged.

"Oh no," Mom says. "I never told anyone."

"Yes you did. You told me."

"I didn't. Why would I tell anyone?"

"Jesus," Benny mutters, shaking his head.

"All right, sure," my father says. "I must've dreamed it
then." I can't understand why my father is so mad. Or is he
frightened, too? Why doesn't he take her hand?

"Mom," I say, "you know this sort of thing affects people
their whole lives."

"Nah," my mother says, and then she laughs.

No matter what I am doing this scene flickers on the far wall
of my mind. My mother is sixteen, dressed for a date, her nails
painted dark red, her coffee-colored hair ratted up two inches
at the crown of her head. Her father has taken off all his clothes.
His skin is papery white. His shriveled white penis is wagging.
Like a thumb. Her father is pinning her against the sink in their
South Side of Chicago kitchen. "Watch out for those Mexicans,
Bebe," he tells her. He has whiskey on his breath. His penis is
rising and wagging like a puppet. He is pressing her against the
sink with his long white bristled body. "I love you, Bebe. I love
you."

Now's the time we should all tell Mom that it's OK. We love her. Instead, everyone is too busy not looking me in the eye, and I am too busy watching them do it. My father's, my mother's, Benny's skin looks sickly yellow in the candlelight. My father hails the waiter, asks for the check, doesn't even order coffee.

We don't talk as we walk between the plaster columns, made to look like the Parthenon, out to the front door of the restaurant. Outside my father stares at me a moment, and I see his face is sagging. Is he sad because of the sad story we just heard, or is it because I am not the daughter he wanted? Would he rather I had a good time tonight, like Miss South Side? I want to say something, but what?

My hands, my fingers, feel as if they're missing. I don't know what to do next. What I need is to be alone to think about all this. There's a store down the street where they sell Greek Orthodox candles. That's what I need. I need a holy candle. I'll wait until they go to sleep tonight, then I'll light it and think and think and think about this. My skin, my face, is numb, and all I want to do is think about this.

"I'll see you at the house," I say, and I start to break away from them.

"Where are you going?" Benny asks me. "You can't walk to your car alone now. It's dark."

"It's OK. Look. There're tons of people on the street."

"We'll drive you to your car," my dad says. He looks so tired. His eyes have lost their color.

"No, I want to stop at a store over there." I point vaguely. I'm moving back into my life without them. I don't want them to know my plans.

"Are you nuts?" Benny says. "It's gotten bad around here. Look at those guys hanging around down there." Three dark-haired men, they appear to be Greek, are standing on the corner. One is sipping from a foam cup.

"Guys drinking coffee. So what. I'm just going down to the candle store on the corner."

"Don't be stupid," Benny says. He's nearly hysterical. "You don't know what it's like living in a big city. You've been gone too long."

"Oh for God's sake," I say, and I start to walk away from them. When I look over my shoulder I see my mother following me.

She seems so small on the wide, dirty sidewalk. "What are you doing?" I ask.

"I want to look at the candles, too."

Sometimes I wonder if I could leave my life, become Miss South Side, thirty pounds thinner, hair blond as the edge of a candle flame, looped up on my head like Aunt Lucy's at her wedding. I see Miss South Side all the time, sometimes even in Minnesota, in shopping malls or in the St. Paul skyways. *Miss South Side of Chicago is in her thirties now. Her blond hair still holds its white highlights. Her legs are smooth under her hose. She wears medium-height pumps and tinted stockings. Her skirt is cut narrow, and her sweater is white and beige with a cowl neck.* I'm wearing leopard-colored leggings, a stretchy cotton skirt, and big black Doc Marten boots. One of my socks has a hole in the heel that I tried to forget by turning the sock around, but watching her I can't forget it's there. *Her fingernails are perfect, painted dark rose today.* Mine are trimmed a little unevenly. *When she walks with her friends, she is the one who is talking, chattering really, filling up all the spaces in the air around her.* Watching her, my face feels too big for my body.

Could I still be her? I examine her as she passes, her pumps snapping on the tile floor. I could leave Linnea, our dog, our three cats, the duplex we decorated together with holy candles and

statues of the Madonna. I could go to another city, get a job in
an office, get a downtown apartment. No one would know me.
I could buy new clothes, pastels and earth tones. I could streak
my hair blond as a lit bulb, grow long bird-beak nails and polish
them red. I could date handsome white men I'd meet at the office or in singles bars. I could get fitted for a diaphragm, follow
make-up tips from *Glamour* and *Cosmo,* buy creams for wrinkles around the eyes, creams for unsightly cellulite. I would never
discuss the past. No one would know me. I could drink white
wine, and red, and Tanqueray tonics, vodka tonics, godmothers
and Tom Collins, chatting with bartenders, perched on the edge
of my supper club chair, gagging if anyone mentioned lezzies,
the smoke from my cigarette spiraling up to the ceiling. I could
be her, the girl my parents wanted, and I could drink, and I could
forget, and pretty soon I would certainly be dead.

I dream of Aunt Lucy, her dyed hair yellow as the edge of
a flame, my hair dyed red as a flame's middle. *You're a beauty
queen,* she says, and reaches out her hand. I take it, and we rise
into the air. We have wings. We fly. *We'll escape to California,*
Aunt Lucy says to me, her yellow hair flickering. California. It
will be warm I think. *Like I did,* Aunt Lucy says to me. *A nice
suburb in Los Angeles. You can get married. Become a Repub-
lican.*

I can't go to California, I say to Aunt Lucy, letting go of her
hand. *I have to tell this story.* I plummet back to the South Side,
my dyed hair flaming red. People below will be afraid when they
look up. I must look like a ball of fire from the end of the world.

"You didn't light that candle in the house?" my mom asks
the next morning when I try to talk to her about her story.

She's closed up, dry, her face blank as a sidewalk. She stands in her bedroom folding laundry, and I am about to leave, to drive back up to Waukegan to meet Linnea so we can go home.

"Mom," I say, "when bad things happen in a family, it affects all of us."

"I don't believe in psychological reasons for things," she says.

"It affects me, Mom."

"What affects you?"

"All of this. Secrets in the family. There're reasons, you know, that I had so much trouble getting my life together."

"Are you saying you have mental problems?" When she says *mental,* her face tightens, like she smells something bad.

"I'm just saying I had some problems, Ma. Like, I used to drink too much."

"You have a problem with drinking?"

"Come on, Ma, you know that. I didn't tell any of you except Paulie and Mitsuko, but you know, don't you?"

"You told Mitsuko?"

At another family dinner I told Mitsuko, at another restaurant in Greektown, when she asked me why I always turn my wineglass over. Her long black hair was fastened back with a silver barrette, and she was tiny next to my six-foot brothers and father. They were talking football, so no one paid attention.

"Sometimes I don't like all the drinking," she whispered to me. Then she turned her glass over too, and my mother noticed that.

"What are you teaching her?" my mother shouted across the table. "Are you teaching her to be strange like you?"

I watch my reflection in the big mirror in my mother's new oak-frame bed. I am so tall that the image of my head bumps against the frame of the mirror. My mother is tiny, more Mitsuko's size. Am I really her daughter? As usual, I am surprised at my reflection. I always expect someone blonder, thinner, not so tall. I'm shocked at how copper my hair is, at my skin tone that Linnea says is the color of clover honey, at my unusual face, its pronounced nose with a bump where it was broken, and my flat Slavic cheeks, my furry, fake leopard vest, my hair cut shorter on the left than the right, and my one long silver earring shaped like a snake. People around here must think I look like Miss South Side of Mars. At the moment, that's exactly what I want them to think. I'd rather be from anywhere but here. But that will pass, and I'll crave a homeland again.

"But you don't drink at all," my mother continues.

"Right, Ma. I stopped drinking. I'm sorry I didn't tell you, but I thought you knew."

"Why would you tell me something like that?" Her face is starting to wrinkle up again, like it did in the restaurant last night.

"I don't know. To get closer?" I feel my face get warm. I'm not accustomed to saying things like that to anyone in my family, but it doesn't matter. She doesn't seem to hear me.

"You used to smoke that stuff. You thought that was OK."

"Right. I've stopped that too."

"Well, that means you're stronger than some people. My father wasn't strong."

"I had to get help. I needed to find out why I was so screwed-up."

"I can't help if that lifestyle of yours makes you screwed-up."

"Ma, it's not that. Can't you see that I'm happy for the first time with Linnea?"

"I'll never stop wishing for you to change." To me this sounds as if she's saying, *Go away, before you turn the whole neighborhood bad.* She opens her dresser drawer, an old brown wood piece, darker than the new bed frame. I used to dust it when I was a kid. My mother sets her neatly folded underwear in the open drawer.

"OK, OK, but this isn't what I wanted to talk about," I say.

What I mean to tell her next, never gets said. That I'm afraid, worried, now that I know, that I will start to remember more about Grandpa. That I will remember the times he touched me.

"What Grandpa did to you, it's important," I say.

"It's in the past. Why think about things that are over?"

"Because they aren't over, Ma. They aren't."

"They are," she says, slamming the drawer closed, turning her back on me, leaving the room.

I'm left alone with the reflection of myself. I stare into my own face and wonder, would she tell me more if I were Miss South Side? Now's the time she's supposed to come back and say that she loves me no matter who I am. But she doesn't.

I stare at myself. The morning light ripples through the copper streaks in my hair. The lighted dial of the clock radio by the bed reads 10:00 A.M. If traffic's bad, it could take two hours to drive north though the stinking mill fields, past downtown, into the northern suburbs. I told Linnea I'd meet her at noon, and I miss her. It's time for me to go home.

restoring the
color of roses

1979

I am at the bar with Anna. Our other roommates, Beth and Renée, are here with us, but they aren't important. The only thing that matters is that I am here with Anna.

1990

Once I start remembering I begin to have trouble making love with Linnea.

Some aching part of me feels exposed, so her mouth on my nipples, her fingers in my cunt, set off a clenching in me.

It used to be I liked her to suck my nipples hard, so hard pain became screaming pleasure, my wet cunt rising to meet her hand. Now, the slightest tug at my breast sets my flesh against her, pulling back, pursing like the tense lips of disapproval, spitting, spitting, away, alone.

1979

"Barrie, want to go to Treno's?" Beth asks. Renée and Beth have their coats on, and Renée is chanting, "Party Hardy, Party

Hardy," stamping her foot, her chin bobbing to the beat.

I can't stand Renée. She always talks, on and on like a fire drill, and when she laughs she's louder than anyone else in the room. She brings home men from bars and has sex with them on the living room sofa, and I feel so embarrassed for her.

I look to Anna, whose books and papers are spread across the round kitchen table. Anna is always studying. I try to study but have trouble concentrating. I read all the novels from my English classes, but mostly I pull things together the night before they're due. Anna is more serious. She's trying to get into Physical Therapy school. She says it's the only thing that matters, aside from her boyfriend Ken who lives three hours away in Chicago and mails her letters every day in green envelopes with cartoons and quotes from poems scratched in the corners. Every time Anna talks about Ken I feel cut in the heart. I want to matter to Anna.

Anna yawns, looking pretty and sleepy. "I could stand a beer," she says, dropping her pencil into the crease of her biology book. I feel a fluttering in my chest. Anna wants to go out.

When Anna goes out, she changes out of her denim work shirt and sweatpants. She wears red, puts on long earrings made of feathers, spreads sparkly brown shadow over her eyelids. Tonight I'm in Levis and my favorite blouse, faded perfectly, with a tiny grease stain in back. Since it's nearly spring, I've got on my red clogs. Sometimes I wear 1940s dresses from the Salvation Army and tights, if I can find them in turquoise or rose, but tonight Anna's dressed casual, red overalls and a black turtleneck, and so I'm dressed casual too. Anna has high cheekbones, eyes the color of frosted blue marbles, skin pale as Ivory soap. I think Anna Maklevich is the most beautiful girl I've ever seen.

At first I only caught glimpses of her. We both lived in Busey Hall. Her room was down the hall from mine. I watched her, secretly, my door open, pretending to be bored, pretending to study, as she passed by on her way back from the bathroom.

When she studied on weekends, she always wore tie-dyed long underwear pants and a stretched-out University of Illinois sweatshirt. Even then I thought she was perfect, a sculpture. I was reading *Anna Karenina* that semester. Anna Maklevich and Anna Karenina were confused in my mind. I'd dream of Anna Karenina in the Russian mist. I stared at Anna Maklevich and my mouth felt so dry I couldn't taste my tongue.

Now I share a room with Anna in a three-room university-chaperoned apartment, three blocks from the bar. *Chaperoned* means the Christian couple, who live on the first floor, check once a month to make sure we've cleaned. One weekend a month Ken comes down from Chicago for the weekend, and I have to sleep on the living room couch. But otherwise I have Anna pretty much to myself. Anna tells me she doesn't really like girls, except for me. When she says that I hear a sound inside myself that makes me shiver, screech, and whirr, the way a freight train sounds if you stand too close to the tracks.

1990

Linnea does not resemble Anna. For one thing, she is not pretty, not in the way the word *pretty* is used. She is too strong to be pretty, too rough and wide, and wrangling. Her brown hair is always cropped close against the side of her head, curling only from the flat-cut top. She admires the young Marlon Brando, has a motorcycle, and looks like a biker: tight jeans, leather jacket, cowboy boots. She wears bolo ties and wide-brimmed hats. Outside, she wears dark glasses. Anna was beautiful, a dream escaped from a Russian novel. Linnea is handsome.

When I started dating Linnea, I expected to find her as butch inside as out. I was stunned the first time I saw her naked. She is not lean and small-breasted like Anna was. Linnea looks like a movie star, the old kind, with big shoulders and breasts so large it seems to me they must hurt. Her body is like Jane Russell's in *Gentlemen Prefer Blondes*. She froze the first time I told her this. She wasn't ready to be that soft with me.

Three years later she is not so afraid. Now I feel soft, and I'm terrified to tell her. How long will I be afraid of her touch? Will she wait? Will she leave?

"Are you mad?" I ask.

"I miss you," she says.

"But are you mad?"

"No, I'm patient."

"But why love me if I can't make love to you?"

"I just love you."

"But why?"

She sighs. "I love you because you're smart, because we talk about our lives together. I love you because you're beautiful to me. I love you because I feel you with me. I can't describe it as well as you can, and I love you for that too. You listen to me. You make me laugh. You're gentle with me. We're silly together. You spoon me in the bed at night. I love you because I feel you in my heart."

"Sometimes I hate myself," I say.

She says, "I know."

1979

At night I lie in bed pretending to sleep, and I watch Anna undress. Anna isn't afraid to be naked in front of me, which is something I admire about her. I'm afraid to be naked in front of anyone. Guys tell me I have nice breasts and good legs, but alone with a mirror I feel nauseated. I'm put together clumsily, too thick in the thighs, my breasts too small and saggy, too puffy in the stomach. Anna's body is long and pale, with a copper tuft between her thighs and dark nipples the color of roses. I've thought about climbing into bed next to her, planting my lips along the high ridge of her collarbone that so perfectly matches the cliffs of her cheeks. Then I yank my mind back and laugh at how weird my thoughts are.

When I was in high school I found a paperback novel in my father's bedroom. It had a part about two women doing it, and I read that section over and over. I asked myself then, *How come only perverse things make me feel sexy?*

When I think these kinds of thoughts about Anna, I say to myself, *You never should have read that book. It warped your mind.*

1990

It didn't really happen the way I tell it here. I don't remember how it happened. How could I? It was eleven years ago, and I was so often drunk.

Were Anna's nipples really like roses? I remember the nipples of my first woman lover. They were pink, tiny and always knobbed, even when she wasn't excited. Linnea's nipples are pale, the color of strawberry yoghurt. I don't remember Anna's nipples. Perhaps if I had, even once, held them tenderly in my mouth I would be able to recall them now, but I never got that close.

I really did watch Anna undress, but what did I think while I watched? I don't remember anything specific, just a hiss, a pleading inside—*I want, I want*—but what did I want? If someone older, someone who suspected, had grabbed me by the shoulders, shook me, and asked, "Barrie, what *do* you want?" I would have shrugged.

Now I reconstruct, and wish it had been different. I wish I had slipped into her bed, traced her ear with my tongue. No, I wish she had climbed into my bed, slipped her long fingers into

my cunt, sucked hard at my nipples which were not the color
of roses, which were more the color of figs.

1979

At the bar we share a pitcher of beer. I worry there won't
be enough, drink fast so I'm sure to get more.

Beth is talking about a girl who admitted, in front of her
whole sociology class, that she was a lesbian. Beth is a skinny
girl with eyes the shape of half dollars, and straight, fine hair
that hangs flat against her head. She twitches when she talks,
her eyes flickering, her fingers drumming the table. Renée laughs
so loud people at the next table turn and stare.

"I don't think it's bad," Beth says. "I just don't understand
how gay people make love." Her enormous, baffled eyes blink.

"Ken told me, in Chicago, he's seen homosexuals having sex
in public bathrooms." Anna twists her lips, like she's sucking
something sour.

"Gross," Renée says.

"We shouldn't be prejudiced," I say. I don't know what I'm
talking about but believe, now that I've said it, that I have to defend my position. I feel twingy in my chair and hear a banging
in my ear.

1990

The banging in my ear—I've heard it intermittently since I
was a small child. Once, when I was twelve, babysitting my little brothers, the sound was so loud I was sure a man was pounding on the basement door with a brick. I was terrified, curled
up on the sofa with a blanket over my head, crying and chok-
ing until at last my parents' key was in the lock. When I heard
their voices I began to suspect the banging was fake, some trick

my brain was playing. Quickly, before they found me crying, I straightened out on the sofa, the blanket over my knees, and pretended to be asleep.

My mother nudged me. "Barrie, come on, get in your own bed." I squinted at my mother's face, lined and shadowy, her eyes distracted, her plastic dangle earrings falling against her cheeks, green snowflakes. "Come on," she repeated. It was clear that she did not hear the banging. She slapped me on the butt, a little too hard. I still heard it, but it was softer now, farther away than the basement.

The banging is rare now. I've since discovered it's due to congestion in my inner ear, aggravated by stress and fear. If I hear it at all it's in the middle of the night when I jerk awake from a dream where I am falling off a high place, a building or cliff.

1979

At the bar I pull myself up in my chair and peer down at the others. "Prejudice is wrong," I say, my voice slicing the air between myself and them.

"Why?" Renée asks, and laughs.

Anna yawns and stands up. She looks so tall and regal, the bar smoke gathering around her head. I expect her to say, *Excuse me, I must go now and meet the Count.*

What she does say is, "I have to pee."

I narrow my eyes at Renée. Beth lights a cigarette, and I stare over her shoulder, out the picture window behind her back. I feel I am dissolving, molecule by molecule. The waitress comes to our table, and I order another pitcher and some popcorn.

Outside, cars swerve through the slushy streets, spraying the window with icy mud. A pack of drunk frat boys stumble by and one presses his face flat against the glass. His cheeks are smashed, his eyes bulged, his lips gross and enormous. A brick is banging, banging against the bolted door of my eardrum.

1990

Our best friend Peter works in a sex toy store.

The night Linnea and I stop by to visit, we find him smoking a cigarette, slumped over a glass case that displays nipple clamps, leather dildos, and studded wrist cuffs. "I'm sick of this place," he says.

"What's this?" I point to a three-inch plastic penis with a metal switch on one side.

Peter flips the switch with his thumb, and a narrow flame shoots up. Deadpan, he says, "Little Dickie Lighter."

I pick up a plastic toy, an ugly rendition of a cunt. I wind it up and set it on the counter. It pops up and down a few times, then falls to the floor. "Jolly Jumping Pussy," Peter explains.

"I would be scared to walk into a house with this stuff on the coffee table," I say.

"Me too," he says. "I wouldn't go out with any of the guys that come in here."

"But would you go *home* with any of them?"

He laughs. "Depends on what they bought."

Linnea is perusing the racks. I find her in front of a display case of battery-operated dildos. Her favorite is a latex sculpture of what looks to be the Virgin Mary. Attached to Mary's feet is another, smaller appendage, in the shape of a cat.

Linnea points to the cat. "Clit Stimulator."

She pushes a red button at the base of the display. The cat vibrates and the Virgin Mary wriggles like a hula dancer.

"Looks like it might work," I say.

"These are like the ones they were selling at the women's music festival," Linnea says, "except those were lavender."

"I can get you twenty percent off," Peter calls from the

front.

"Want to?" Linnea whispers.

"I'm not sure I'd like it," I whisper back, "with the problem I've been having."

"Maybe it'll help." She grins and wriggles her eyebrows. "And it's twenty percent off."

Linnea leaves the store ahead of me, carrying the dildo in a plain paper sack. I hang back and whisper to Peter, "I hope she doesn't want to use it tonight. I'm still afraid to have sex."

"She'll be OK," he whispers back. "She's always telling me how much she loves you."

"Really, she tells you that?" Hearing this excites me. I tend to believe things like this more when I hear them secondhand.

"She says it all the time," he says. "I love your relationship."

"I do too," I say. "I feel grown up with her. I feel married. I'm just so afraid I'll screw it up. I'm so afraid I'll never get out of this mood."

We pick up batteries on the way home, but put the dildo away in a drawer as soon as we get there. A few nights later I slip it into the bed with me, hide it under the covers. When Linnea pulls back the quilt I hit the switch. She yelps and falls back. The dildo, exposed, wriggles alone.

I laugh so hard I accidently kick it out of the bed. It wriggles across the floor like a centipede. The buzzing attracts the dog, who noses it and growls.

Linnea picks it up. It squirms, alive in her hand.

"You look like the snake goddess," I say.

"It's covered with cat hair," she says.

"You could wash it."

"Does that mean you want to try it?"

"I don't know. What if it feels like a penis?"

"Can a penis do this?" She switches it to high.

"Not in my experience," I say.

She flips it off and wipes away the cat hair. Then she flips it on again and pounces onto the bed. I giggle when she pokes the Virgin's head into my side. "That tickles."

Then she pushes it against my crotch, and I come immediately, right through my underpants. My orgasm is like an electric shock.

"It didn't feel like making love," I say later. "Do you think it was?"

"No," she says, "that wasn't making love."

1979

These guys are at the table, Tom and Joe and Gary, no—Joe, Gary, Tom, or John, or, hee, I don't know. They bought the last pitcher. This one guy, Gary or Tom, says he's a professor of engineering. Everything he says is the funniest thing I ever heard.

This beer is so smooth, soft as soup going in me. I put one glass down on the table and see two glasses. This is so funny. The beer comes out of nowhere, a spigot in the air filling and filling my glass. My lips tingle as I gulp, ah, my whole body is smooth, no, it's rough, tossing water over rocks. Ha. I love. . .what? I . . . I just love.

Who are these guys? The one, Professor Gary, has a crinkly beard. Looks like pubic hair, I'm thinking, and I giggle and spit my beer. Then Anna, her face is all eyes and she's staring at me. Those blue marble eyes are enormous, glassy. *Anna, Anna, what is it?* I am beached, shivering. Anna hates me. I can see this in those gigantic glass eyes. *O God, Anna, please don't hate me!*

Anna stands up and says "Good night." Then pop, she's vanished. Where did she go, just like that, in a pop? She's gone now, but the glass eyes are still here, scowling at me. Or maybe she left before, hours ago. Or maybe it was Renée who left before. Hee. What time is it anyway?

Professor Gary is tugging my arm. Beth is tugging my arm.

She blinks, "You need to pee?" Time hiccups and I am on the toilet, peeing and peeing. I yell to Beth over the jiggling wall of the stall. "Beth, Beth, I think I'm a little drunk." We giggle.

Splashing cold water on my face I say to Beth, "I think I'm too drunk. I think I won't drink anymore tonight." The water clears my head for a moment. I see Beth looking at me in the mirror. "What?" I say.

"Don't go with that guy," she says. "His friend told me he treats girls bad." All six of Beth's eyes blink, one after another, fluttering, fluttering hummingbirds. How pretty, I think.

1990

In the dream I am raped repeatedly. I am trapped in a car at night. The light is liquid blue, and the man's penis feels like a knife in my cunt. As I dream it I think, *Why am I dreaming this?* I already know how it feels to be raped repeatedly.

When I wake I think of that house in the center of a deserted farm and the man with the crinkly black beard who fucked me repeatedly until gray dawn exposed the crumpled winter cornfields.

1979

Outside the bar slush seeps up around my clogs. My socks are wet. Someone passes me a joint. As I inhale, the ember fills my palm with an orange glow so beautiful I cry a little.

Professor Gary pinches my elbow and whispers something into my ear, and I giggle, even though I can't hear what he's saying. *Hiccup,* and I am in a car. Professor Gary is driving. I'm leaning my head back against the seat, looking up. Professor Gary is grumbling and punching the buttons on the radio. The radio static sends little pins up the insides of my legs. He finds a station and the song lyrics, *All we are is dust in the wind,* punch me in the heart. They're so familiar, but I can't think of what they remind me of. The street lamps all run together, string rivers of light, a shimmering highway running just over our heads. *Hiccup.* We are in a bed. He is unbuttoning my shirt and crooning in my ear, "Oh baby, are you sure you're only nineteen?" His pubic hair beard scratches my chin.

1990

When I recall that night, my chest tightens, my throat closes, sometimes my body jerks. How many more times? I can't recall how I felt then, just pictures, just random sensations, just the used rubbers falling like skinned fish around the wide wood bed.

1979

I am watching myself from above. My body is narrow, all one width. My hands, running up and down his hairy back, look stiff as crab claws.

He rocks in and out of me. From above he looks like one of those plastic buoys used to mark off swimming beaches, bobbing and bobbing, bobbing in, bobbing in me, how many more times?

How many guys is it now? There was the lacrosse player in Syracuse. I was so drunk that night I never even felt it. There was the the skinny guy with the big black eyes from the Revolutionary Student Brigade. We did it on a towel, on the floor in Beth and Renée's room the night they were both gone, because Anna was in my room with Ken. There was the guy with the vinyl couch I met in that crummy Illinois State bar, with the dorm room that overlooked downtown Normal. I don't think Anna knows about that one. Then there was that conductor on the train who smuggled me beers because I was underage, but he doesn't count because we just made out. I told Anna about him. She called me a daredevil. Who else? Lots. I can't remember them all. I hope I get to liking it soon. It's good Professor Gary keeps doing it. My muscles down there will stretch, and then I'll start to like it. This is experience. Why am I holding myself so still? Move more, move more, hips arch, *ohh*, this seems a good place to moan. He whispers, "Oh baby, you're good."

Two cool blue discs spin over the bed, the colored spots I see when I clench my eyelids shut. They look like Anna's eyes. I'll bet I'm better at this than her. I'll bet she never slept with a professor, I'll bet, *ow*, God, how many times can this guy get it up? I wonder if he cleans up those rubbers, or just lets them pile up behind the headboard, all gross and gumming together. I think of that "Creature Feature" movie, the woman's severed head kept alive with flasks and tubes while the scientist tries to find her a new body. The scientist tosses spare body parts into a closet until they grow together, a monster who breaks down the closet door. Professor Gary grunts and pulls out of me again. He presses his prickly beard into my stomach. I think I should stroke his head, but I can't move my hands and fingers. From above I coach: sigh now, reach for him, stroke his shoulders, but my fingers feel frostbitten.

He pulls off his rubber and tosses it over the bedpost. Maybe a gummy condom monster will push through the bedsprings, tumble our bodies, Professor Gary's pale skin with the scraggy black hairs smacking the unfinished wood floor, my nude olive skin scraping against the bed frame, while the monster smothers us both with the mattress. Would Anna look for me?

Professor Gary is hard again. He doesn't seem to notice that I am lifeless, completely frostbitten. He rolls on another rubber. He pushes apart my thighs and sticks it in me again. It stings. How many more times?

1990

Linnea shakes me. She does it gently, to make me laugh. She grabs my shoulders and shakes me as if I were tiny, as if I were a child. My head bobs forward and back. I giggle. Linnea grins, then purses her lips, grins and purses again. She looks so funny. The laughing comes out of my stomach.

All week I have been remembering drinking. It's easier than remembering a sting in my cunt from eleven years ago. Why not drink, if abstaining means my skin is always alight with these thousands of prickles and prods from the past? I fantasize holding a bottle of wine to my lips, letting the sharp liquid shiver down my throat until my cells jump apart, until my body lies inert on the floor, numb and stupid.

I haven't been telling this to Linnea. Telling, I might not get to do it. Finally, feeling my hands and head slipping over the brink, I say, "Linnea, I want to drink."

It's not what she wants to hear. I lay on the couch while she sits on the edge, her buttocks pressing into my side. I watch the blinds in her eyes fall closed, *snap snap.* I was two years white-knuckle dry when I met her. She was shocked the night, two years later, when she came home and found me drunk. I had finished a fifth of vodka in an hour and a half. She wanted to leave, take the dog, stay with a friend, away from me. She remained to take my pulse every fifteen minutes, to make sure alcohol poisoning wouldn't stop my heart, to make sure I wouldn't die.

A year has passed. I had treatment. Still, there are times I believe it was all a mistake. I'm no alcoholic. I can drink. I can drink for days. These are the times that I crave not just alcohol but my old life, the blur and rush, the mess, and the constant, bitter laughing that came out of the raw spot just under my tongue.

Linnea stuck with me through one relapse. She won't promise to stay through another. Still, I want to drink. No, I don't want to drink. I can't have the old life and this one too. I am in hand-to-hand combat with myself.

"Maybe you should call someone," she offers.

"I wish you'd been my roommate then," I say. "Instead of Anna. Then we'd have fallen in love years ago and I could have skipped so much shit."

"I wouldn't have fallen in love with you then."

"You would've," I flirt. I pinch her side and she pulls away further. "You wouldn't have been able to help it."

"I wouldn't have been with a drunk."

A drunk? It still horrifies me to admit it. Grandpa Luschak was the drunk. Everyone knows that. That's why his face was so prickly, his hands always so cold. Remembering Grandpa, I feel him alive in the cavities of my body and my skin puckers, pulls away from my bones.

"Are you on Anna's side?" Fear makes me petulant. Is she getting ready to leave me?

"What's Anna's side? I'm talking about myself."

"I didn't know I was a drunk. How would you have known? We didn't know about those things then."

"My father was the last drunk I'll ever live with. I would have known."

"But everyone drinks in college."

"You told me you drank every day. I didn't drink every day. My friends didn't drink every day."

"I was a kid. I was confused."

"You were really young," she agrees.

"Everyone's fucked up when they're nineteen."

"Everyone doesn't end up in chem dep treatment when they're thirty."

"Do you hate me for that?"

"No, no." She sighs, frustrated. "You've been working so hard. We're both changing."

"How are you changing?"

"I can tell you my feelings."

"What are you feeling right now?"

"I feel dizzy. You ask too many questions." I'm pushing her, I know. I'm wearing her out, but I can't stop asking. The questions are driving me closer, to what?

"Did treatment make me boring?"

"I like you better now. You pay more attention to me."

"But I'm afraid to make love."

"I'll wait."

She's still sitting next to me, but I can't feel her body. My senses are blocked. "Do you think that professor raped me?" I ask.

"You were drunk, and a kid, a student. Suppose you were him, today. Suppose you picked up some young cute girl in a bar who was too drunk to know what she was doing. Suppose you gave her drugs, then took her to some secluded place, some place she wouldn't know how to get home from, then stripped her and did things to her naked body all night."

I shrug, and that's when she shakes me. I don't know why she thinks of it. She reaches over, pulls me up from the couch and shakes. Her face looks ridiculous, too large, out of focus. The laughing comes out of my stomach. I don't want to drink. I want to love her.

But I can't stop remembering that man, his penis. It still feels like my fault.

1979

I find this letter when I get home.

> *I wish you would clean up your side of the fucking room. I wish you wouldn't leave your typewriter in the kitchen. I wish you wouldn't use my loofah bath mitt. I wish, just once, on your way to the fuck-*

ing bar, you'd remember to stop and buy toilet pa-
per. When I got back after that weekend you were
here alone and I saw there was no toilet paper, I was
embarrassed for you. I wish you'd wash some fuck-
ing dishes. When I first moved in with you I
thought, Barrie's so cool. I don't mind cleaning her
dishes. Now I mind. I wish you'd remember to turn
off your electric blanket. I wish you'd stop coming
home drunk and knocking over all the lamps. I
wish you weren't such a slut.   *Anna*

No one is home but me. I've got "The Low Spark of High Heeled Boys" playing loud on the stereo, but still that brick is pounding against the basement door. I need a shower. Professor Gary asked me if I wanted one, but I think he meant I should take it with him. By then I was only a little bit drunk, and nauseated besides. I was too embarrassed to stand in the bathroom naked where he could see me upright. I put on my clothes while he was showering. He must have thought I was gross, putting on my clothes when I was still sticky from him. He grabbed my breasts through my shirt and asked why I didn't wear a bra. I said I just didn't like bras, but I don't know if that's the truth.

I want to be telling all this to Anna, but it looks like that's impossible now. It's so stupid of me to forget to buy toilet paper. Still, she must be crazy to get so mad about it. God, I hope the others never come home. I want to lie here alone, forever. I need a shower. I must stink. My head is swimming. God, I wish this pounding in my ears would stop.

Many years. Always.

The used rubbers fell like skinned fish around the wide wood bed. He raped me repeatedly. When did I start to know it was rape? There was never one moment, and none of this happened the way I tell it here. How could it? Memory is much too imaginary. Linnea doesn't understand why I have so much trouble knowing what is true. We're different that way.

1990

Linnea and I do make love again. It has been three months. I don't remember all the details, but it goes something like this.

She's lying in bed next to me, reading a book for her dissertation, something about the making of homosexual community. "Want to do some real research?" I say.

She looks up from her book. "Really?"

I pull off my shirt, lean over her, suck the soft flesh at the base of her neck. Her book drops to the floor. I try to take off her glasses, but the bows are stuck behind her ears, so she helps me. She rolls over on top of me and kisses me hard. I say, "Take this off," and yank her shirt up over her head.

I am pretending this is easy. I do feel a pull, a hotness between my breasts, but the rest of my body is still numb. There is a moment that I lie frozen. Will I thaw? Will I prickle away from her? She pulls me close, wraps her arms around the sensitive plane between my breasts and my waist. I thaw.

Her breasts, larger and more tender than mine, press into me, and I wrap my thighs around her thighs. We rock, kissing and tonguing each others' necks and ears. My body begins to tremble, slightly, a rustling. It is the love that rushes to my mouth, the knowing that my most burnt and huddled self is safe here. "Linnea, Linnea, I've missed you so much."

She sucks my nipple, a little too hard, and I whisper, "Gentle, gentle." My body tenses. My body shakes. My breath squeaks out in hot patches. I try to roll over on top of her, but she pushes me back down against the pillows.

"Stay right here," she whispers. A high tension wire is strung from my head to my cunt. I groan and open my thighs.

When she slips her finger inside me my cunt is already slippery. I open my eyes to look at her face. She wears the expression I love the most—serious, driven, starved. Her eyes fix on my face, she breathes fast and hard, her lips taste the salt of my damp skin. I'm caught up in her desire for me, and in the throbbing of my own nipples and cunt, so only part of me leaves my body, for a moment, to think, *This is how it feels to be wanted, but not just my body. Those men who fucked and fucked me never even wondered who was inside. This is how it feels for all of me to be wanted.*

She slips two more fingers into my cunt and everything flashes deep blue. No more thinking. I let out a guttural yelp, and my body, myself, collapses around her pulsing hand. My hips jerk, and then I am quiet, closing my thighs around her forearm, pulling her heavy chest to mine, sinking my face into the downy field of her hair.

1990

I dream Anna comes back to see me.

"I didn't know I was a drunk," I tell her. I hear the brick beating. I unbutton my shirt, bare my chest to her. "I wasn't a slut. I just loved you."

Anna stares at me, those marble eyes spinning. Her irises are the color of hurricanes. Her skin looks clear and stinging as sleet. She says nothing.

I lean into her face, watch my reflection spin in her eyes. Still, she is silent.

"Anna," I hiss, "you are a bitch."

This startles me awake. Linnea sleeps beside me, breathing hotly into her pillow, her fingers relaxed, curled into her palm.

Her fists look like rosebuds. I kiss her forehead. She moans sweetly but does not wake up.

Other titles from Firebrand Books include:

Artemis In Echo Park, Poetry by Eloise Klein Healy/$8.95

Beneath My Heart, Poetry by Janice Gould/$8.95

The Big Mama Stories by Shay Youngblood/$8.95

The Black Back-Ups, Poetry by Kate Rushin/$8.95

A Burst Of Light, Essays by Audre Lorde/$8.95

Cecile, Stories by Ruthann Robson/$8.95

Crime Against Nature, Poetry by Minnie Bruce Pratt/$8.95

Diamonds Are A Dyke's Best Friend by Yvonne Zipter/$9.95

Dykes To Watch Out For, Cartoons by Alison Bechdel/$7.95

Dykes To Watch Out For: The Sequel, Cartoons by Alison Bechdel/$8.95

Exile In The Promised Land, A Memoir by Marcia Freedman/$8.95

Eye Of A Hurricane, Stories by Ruthann Robson/$8.95

The Fires Of Bride, A Novel by Ellen Galford/$8.95

Food & Spirits, Stories by Beth Brant (*Degonwadonti*)/$8.95

Free Ride, A Novel by Marilyn Gayle/$9.95

A Gathering Of Spirit, A Collection by North American Indian Women
edited by Beth Brant (*Degonwadonti*)/$10.95

Getting Home Alive by Aurora Levins Morales and Rosario Morales/$9.95

The Gilda Stories, A Novel by Jewelle Gomez/$9.95

Good Enough To Eat, A Novel by Lesléa Newman/$8.95

Humid Pitch, Narrative Poetry by Cheryl Clarke/$8.95

Jewish Women's Call For Peace edited by Rita Falbel, Irena Klepfisz, and
Donna Nevel/$4.95

Jonestown & Other Madness, Poetry by Pat Parker/$7.95

Just Say Yes, A Novel by Judith McDaniel/$8.95

The Land Of Look Behind, Prose and Poetry by Michelle Cliff/$8.95

Legal Tender, A Mystery by Marion Foster/$9.95

Lesbian (Out)law, Survival Under the Rule of Law by Ruthann Robson
/$9.95

A Letter To Harvey Milk, Short Stories by Lesléa Newman/$8.95

Letting In The Night, A Novel by Joan Lindau/$8.95

Living As A Lesbian, Poetry by Cheryl Clarke/$7.95

Making It, A Woman's Guide to Sex in the Age of AIDS by Cindy Patton
and Janis Kelly/$4.95

Metamorphosis, Reflections On Recovery by Judith McDaniel/$7.95

Mohawk Trail by Beth Brant (*Degonwadonti*)/$7.95

Moll Cutpurse, A Novel by Ellen Galford/$7.95

The Monarchs Are Flying, A Novel by Marion Foster/$8.95

More Dykes To Watch Out For, Cartoons by Alison Bechdel/$7.95

Movement In Black, Poetry by Pat Parker/$8.95

My Mama's Dead Squirrel, Lesbian Essays on Southern Culture by Mab
Segrest/$9.95

New, Improved! Dykes To Watch Out For, Cartoons by Alison Bechdel/$7.95

The Other Sappho, A Novel by Ellen Frye/$8.95

Out In The World, International Lesbian Organizing by Shelley Anderson /$4.95

Politics Of The Heart, A Lesbian Parenting Anthology edited by Sandra Pollack and Jeanne Vaughn/$12.95

Presenting. . .Sister NoBlues by Hattie Gossett/$8.95

Rebellion, Essays 1980-1991 by Minnie Bruce Pratt/$10.95

A Restricted Country by Joan Nestle/$9.95

Running Fiercely Toward A High Thin Sound, A Novel by Judith Katz /$9.95

Sacred Space by Geraldine Hatch Hanon/$9.95

Sanctuary, A Journey by Judith McDaniel/$7.95

Sans Souci, And Other Stories by Dionne Brand/$8.95

Scuttlebutt, A Novel by Jana Williams/$8.95

Shoulders, A Novel by Georgia Cotrell/$8.95

Simple Songs, Stories by Vickie Sears/$8.95

Speaking Dreams, Science Fiction by Severna Park/$9.95

Stone Butch Blues, A Novel by Leslie Feinberg/$10.95

The Sun Is Not Merciful, Short Stories by Anna Lee Walters/$8.95

Talking Indian, Reflections on Survival and Writing by Anna Lee Walters /$10.95

Tender Warriors, A Novel by Rachel Guido deVries/$8.95

This Is About Incest by Margaret Randall/$8.95

The Threshing Floor, Short Stories by Barbara Burford/$7.95

Trash, Stories by Dorothy Allison/$9.95

We Say We Love Each Other, Poetry by Minnie Bruce Pratt/$8.95

The Women Who Hate Me, Poetry by Dorothy Allison/$8.95

Words To The Wise, A Writer's Guide to Feminist and Lesbian Periodicals & Publishers by Andrea Fleck Clardy/$5.95

The Worry Girl, Stories from a Childhood by Andrea Freud Loewenstein /$8.95

Yours In Struggle, Three Feminist Perspectives on Anti-Semitism and Racism by Elly Bulkin, Minnie Bruce Pratt, and Barbara Smith/$8.95

You can buy Firebrand titles at your bookstore, or order them directly from the publisher (141 The Commons, Ithaca, New York 14850, 607-272-0000).

Please include $2.00 shipping for the first book and $.50 for each additional book.

A free catalog is available on request.